# CONTENTS

A sale in progress at Christie's, London

## THE LURE OF COLLECTING

Is there something akin to gambling in the collecting of works of art, or is there a deeper feeling that seizes the mind? The passion is not a new one, writers from the past record many incidents of both public and private collections that date back to the early Egyptians. It was Ptolemy Soter who ruled Alexandria and built what was probably the first museum there in 280 BC. The tastes of the early enthusiasts seem to have been as wide as ours are today. The early Hellenistic kings (c. 283–133 BC) went after not only paintings, but sculpture, books, and precious jewels. Much of the early collecting was probably done as a side activity to conquests. Today the animating process is the same, but the means of procuring are perhaps a little gentler.

### Spectacular auctions

For most, the word 'collecting' brings to mind one of the great salerooms of the world. It is to these establishments

Hamlyn all-colour paperbacks

John FitzMaurice Mills

# Collecting & Looking After Antiques

**Hamlyn**
London · New York · Sydney · Toronto

# FOREWORD

The collecting of works of art and antiques is fast becoming a compulsion. At one end of the scale it can be a very costly business, but at the other there is plenty of scope. The ideal way of setting about it is to get in at the start of a trend, even possibly to sense out a trend for oneself. Today there seems no limit to the objects that will be tomorrow's 'collectors' pieces'. Good money is being paid for yesterday's commercial labels, old dairy utensils, and for, believe it or not, such unlikely things as old barbed wire.

However, this book is primarily about how to look after the antiques you have taken the trouble to collect. Although the seriously damaged objects should always be left to the expert restorer, there is much that can be done to prevent, or help cure, the maladies which may occur. As well as what to do, advice has been given here as to what *not* to do. If in doubt, do not rush blindly on, as did the owner of an exquisite Japanese ivory carving who believed it to be in a very dirty state and took a tin of bath-scouring powder and a piece of rag and very quickly brought up a burnished white surface on the ivory, remarking that all those 'coloured stains' had now been got rid of. Unfortunately she was not aware that the 'stains' were the intentional colouring of the original carver. How very easy it is to mar a beautiful piece but often quite impossible to do anything about it when the damage has been done.

J.F.M.

Published by The Hamlyn Publishing Group Limited
London · New York · Sydney · Toronto
Astronaut House, Feltham, Middlesex, England

Copyright © The Hamlyn Publishing Group Limited 1973
Fourth impression 1977

ISBN 0 600 31723 4
Phototypeset by BAS Printers Limited, Wallop, Hampshire
Colour separations by Schwitter Limited, Zurich
Printed in Spain by Mateu Cromo, Madrid

that come not only a large part of the total antique sales, but also the dealers, the curious and, of course, the collectors. Well controlled publicity can assist not only in the creating of the right atmosphere, but produce cliff-hanging suspense as the auctioneer's voice intones its way to an expected record figure – close up to £2,000,000 – for a few square feet of canvas with a thin layer of pigment, a coat of priming, a wooden stretcher and a handful of tacks!

## Evaluating a work of art

Can a truly accurate price be put on a work of art, whether it is in the top flight with a Velasquez or whether it is some humble trinket which attracts the eye? The answer must be in the negative. Works of hand and skill cannot be equated to a value in the same way as a pound of butter or a sack of corn. Even with the commonest categories there will inevitably be a degree of rarity value and this brings into action the old law of supply and demand. Other factors that can

Velasquez's *Juan de Pareja*, sold at Christie's for £2,310,000

cause a ripple through the scene include fashion that can bring on very considerable fluctuations in the market. Intense demand will encourage the work of the forger; the mere sound of the word 'forgery' brings a chill to the heart of some bidders. It need not follow that all replicas that appear were necessarily produced in the first place with the intention of deceiving. Probably the great majority were quite innocently commissioned as copies, even when made centuries ago.

Authentification and provenance are two complex fields. For the novice collector the safest advice is to fasten on to the trail with the determination of a bloodhound. Study the particular line, read and observe. From this course will come the backing for the most important characteristic of intuition.

There is a wealth of wonder and fascination in the field of

A fine French Rococo commode

The scene at an Irish auction

collecting. There is the appreciation of the long done work of some craftsman coupled with a love of the materials he has used. There can be the added piquancy of previous owners and their escapades. But perhaps most of all there is the subtle satisfaction for the aesthetic yearning that is in all of us; a sense of mutual enjoyment with the artist or designer who brought this object, with which we have fallen in love, into being.

## Country sales and auctions

The tryst may take place at any time once the pursuit has started. For many the first introduction to what can become almost a totally absorbing career may be the small country sale. In varying guises these fast-talking showpieces take place almost all over the world. The language may be different, the objects may vary, but the breathless tense bidders will all look much the same.

Where possible always take advantage of the 'viewing' days before the sale day as this will provide some chance to assess possible items. Take time to examine. Remember, that

Objects being assembled before a sale

once the sale starts the pace will be hot, most 'lots' being disposed of in under a minute, and there will be no time for decision-making. It may sound elementary, but always find out auctioneers' rates of commission, and also, who is liable to pay for what. For although in most cases commission will be paid to the saleroom by the seller, there may be instances where the buyer may find himself liable. If you are selling, be quite sure that you understand the ruling with regard to the placing of a reserve on a lot, and what will happen if that figure is not reached.

The major salerooms publish catalogues well ahead of sale dates. These can in some cases be so comprehensive and well illustrated that they are works of reference in their own right. But again they may need a little special understanding. A picture labelled, as for example, by: 'Sir Joshua Reynolds' could be expected to be an entirely genuine and fine example by this master; on the other hand, a painting claiming to be 'Reynolds' could be taken as being in doubt, or by some of the artist's assistants.

## Junk shops

A junk shop, where the windows are piled with bric-à-brac, the inside is stacked with folios – even today, after all the raking through that must have been given – can still come up with the unexpected. One conscientious seeker, not long ago, fumbled through a cobweb-bound folder of worthless prints, to come across an aquatint by Picasso. It is the *possibility* that drives the searcher on.

## How old is an 'antique'?

Conveniently, for some, the cut-out date for antiques and saleable 'bygones' seems constantly to be advancing. One of the top auction rooms now has a department that is devoting itself to the sale of objects that date up to 1935. This is a cautionary note, as well, for the spring-cleaning enthusiast to be mighty careful what is thrown away. As the supplies from the eighteenth-century, Victorian times and pre First World War dry up, it can quickly become the vogue to collect items from the art movements of the 1920s. Yesterday's cycle lamp has become a curio. The *avant-garde*

Collector's delight – a corner of a junk shop

ornament combined with a mass-produced figure can fetch a number of times more than the original price. Costumes worn by even quite a young grandmother will be on some collector's shopping list.

## Removing grime from paintings

Dirt and grime can hide much. Heavy brown layers of varnish can almost totally obscure the details of a painting. In the upstairs room of a public hall there rested a thin panel against a fireplace. For sixty years it had been used as a fire screen. Adze marks showed that it had been worked a considerable time ago. When it was turned round, the surface was shown to be badly blistered by the heat, but despite this, it was just possible to make out a faint outline of something in the way of a painting. The picture was shown to a top saleroom expert, who passed it off as of no interest. When the painting was subjected to careful cleaning, it was found that, fortunately, most of the blistering was only in the thick layers of varnish; as this came away, there emerged the fine head and shoulders of St Jerome by the Flemish painter, Gaspar de Craeyer, who had once been very much admired by Rubens.

Treasures sometimes lurk under layers of dust and dirt

Most towns in Britain have a group of antique shops

End-piece for this story is that the rediscovered picture was worth in the neighbourhood of £13,000.

## Fakes

Dark tarnish can make silver almost unrecognizable; stains and plain greasy dirt can cover the fine patina of valuable wood. Remember that, as the reverse to all this, the unscrupulous vendor can just as easily apply seeming age by the use of various devices. For example, a cheap tawdry print can be stuck on to canvas and then given several coats of dark tinted varnish. The ways of 'ageing' furniture are legion.

In fifty years from now the problem of being sure is going to be further aggravated by the 'reproduction' piece. Today a fashion has sprung up for this type of furniture and, to a lesser degree, object. This may to a large extent be because of the rarity and price of the 'real', but not entirely.

## Antiques, antiques, everywhere

Looking down the main shopping street of some towns and villages, it almost appears as though there must be nearly one antique emporium for every buyer. The eager salesman is

A well stocked and nicely arranged antique shop

'having a go' all over the place. One of the last pieces of habitation that can be seen on the approach to the bare glaciated wastes of the Hardanger Plateau in Norway proudly swings a tradesman's sign to welcome the enthusiast. A farm gate in the back of beyond holds a giant blackened cauldron painted with a legend to draw the enthusiast off the road and up the track to try his luck.

## The antique shop

The shop run by the dealer who knows his stuff may often specialize in a particular period or division of antiques. The wares will be displayed with care and thought, and normally the pieces will be gleaming and clean, in contrast to those in the saleroom, which are often left deliberately dirty. If you are after a bargain here, your chance is slimmer than at an auction or in a junk shop. The objects in many cases will have themselves been bought by the dealer from a saleroom and will have been well and truly examined.

The owners of the top bracket establishments will often

be recognized authorities in their chosen subjects and on intimate terms with their regular customers.

The quality to be found in the best of London, New York, or Munich shops will be very high indeed as, needless to say, will be the prices. Objects of great rarity, fit for the prize case in a museum, can be on offer. These can include not only what are normally termed 'antiques' but also 'antiquities', which can be drawn from the earliest civilizations.

## Why do we collect?

The reasons why we collect are not just simply for aesthetic satisfaction or for monetary gain. The latter may motivate part of the field, but the real addict is driven on by something much more complex. It is perhaps a compound of association with history, skill, beauty, interest, materials, and to an indefinable degree, mystery. No collector, if asked, could probably give a satisfactory answer. He would put forward reasons which would, in all likelihood, be argued by the next man. There is only one undeniable factor which runs through all of us collectors. It is our complete and growing fascination for surrounding ourselves with treasures which have, in many cases, once been other people's treasures.

A display of Chinese blue-and-white porcelain, sixteenth-eighteenth centuries

(*left*) Chairs are popular with beginner-collectors, as well as being useful

(*opposite*) Fine European armour is rare and expensive

## WHAT TO COLLECT?

The whole world of antiques is so diverse. How does one start to put together a collection? If you scatter your shot over the whole scene you may hit lucky, but the serious follower of the rare and beautiful will probably go after one field.

### Furniture

For many, pleasures can be found with furniture. Yet here again this subject is so huge and far-ranging that it must be sub-divided. In England, the Middle Ages until the Restoration was the time for the use of oak. This was followed by the use of mahogany and then walnut, with all the intricate crafts of veneering, marquetry and parquetry. On the Continent were elaborations with the use of gesso and gilding. Oriental vogues for lacquering were emulated. Whereas the furniture from the past in Europe tended towards decorative and opulent forms, the examples of truly American antique furniture can be noted for a more functional approach.

## Arms and armour

Arms and armour have a particular fascination for some. Although they may as a group represent the more brutal side of history, at the same time there is woven into their story elements of chivalry, courage and great deeds. Also, many specimens exhibit some of the highest degrees of the craftsman's skill.

Armour for the protection of the body goes far back into history. The early Greeks used bronze helmets and greaves, (leg guards). The Romans had a liking for a cuirass that was shaped to the chest and the back.

The lines of demarcation between the various periods of body armour are as strongly marked as the varying fashions for dress. The eleventh and twelfth centuries were the time for a tunic of mail for the body and hose of the same material. During the fourteenth and fifteenth centuries was the peak of armour design; it marked the transition from mail to the elaborate system of a covering of plates, engineered with great skill to allow the movement of the wearer, and in the finest examples the armour was decorated with precious metals and consummate artistry.

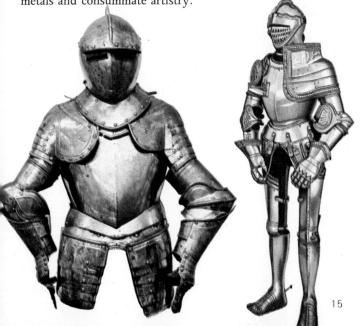

## Cut and thrust weapons

Swords and daggers date back to before 2000 BC. The exact difference between the two is difficult to define, as there are examples of short swords and long daggers. However, the intended use of the weapon can be a guide. The sword is associated with open combat, whilst the dagger is often of a size that can be concealed on the person and used for secret attack.

Asiatic weapons complicate the picture further, the shapes and types having considerable variety. The development of the crescent-shaped scimitar was not from an artistic point of view, but as an aid to its cutting efficiency. The early makers of these weapons worked out that the curved blade would present a more acute cutting edge than a straight sword, and one that could still be applied with the maximum power.

Wars and distant conquests have brought much cross fertilization of shapes with blades and hilts. Both of these and scabbards have lent themselves, at times, to exquisite decoration.

An elaborately decorated
French eighteenth-century sword

A Scottish flintlock belt pistol

## Firearms

The discovery of gunpowder, which it is almost certain took place in the East, brought the introduction of guns, although it is, in fact, likely that these were a Western invention. The early firearms were little more than barrels on wooden poles, which were ignited with a smouldering match held in the other hand.

One of the crossroads in hand-firearms came with the *petronal* or *petrinal*. This was a type of short arquebus, which holds a place midway between the full-sized arquebus and the pistol proper. The petronal was designed so that the butt rested against the chest when it was being fired, and it was fitted with a match- or wheel-lock, a weapon popular in the late sixteenth and seventeenth centuries with horse soldiers.

The 'revolver', as known today, has its home in America, where in 1835 the first practical example was produced by S. Colt. During the Crimean War, both Colt and Adams revolvers were used. During the American Civil war whole corps were armed with up to four revolvers per man.

(*left*) An eighteenth-century wine bottle, with its seal-marking

(*opposite*) A sailor's love token, made of glass

## Glass

One of the most outstanding periods for the production of exquisite glass vessels was the time between the eleventh and the sixteenth century, with Venice as the great centre. The production gradually spread over Europe, and in the sixteenth century 'Venetian Glass' was made in London. The English glass of the eighteenth century holds a high place, particularly the flint-glass, which had a higher degree of brilliance than the Bohemian glass and lent itself to cutting.

Today even the most humble glass objects can command a good figure, as illustrated by the following story. A countryman out ferreting rabbits reached down a burrow to grab his prey, when his hand touched, not something soft and furry, but a smooth cold round shape. He pulled it out and found he was holding an old, round, green bottle with a seal-marking of 1718. How it got there can only be conjectured. The place was several miles from the nearest house, way up on a lonely moor. Perhaps some long-ago roisterer had thrown it down as he rode home. The countryman was not only satisfied, but amazed when he received a sum of about £90 from a saleroom.

## Paperweights

Glass has been used for centuries for producing off-beat objects that could display the skill of the craftsman; one of the most skilled operations being the making of paperweights. With these the coloured patterns were often made by the manipulation of coloured canes. This was generally done either with several of the coloured canes being heated so that they would stick together, or with a single rod that was dipped in varying coloured molten glasses.

## Rolling-pins

One favourite with many are rolling-pins. These first made their appearance during the Napoleonic wars as salt holders. The earlier ones were made from bottle glass, then later came examples of coloured glass, which was usually mottled and striped. Often they were gilded and inscribed with good wishes, bible quotations and mottoes.

## Cut glass

One of the most famous centres for cut glass has been Waterford, in Ireland. The *Dublin Journal* in 1729 notes: 'a glasshouse near Waterford now producing all sorts of flint-glass, double and single . . . sold at reasonable rates by Joseph Harris at Waterford, merchant.' But it was not until 1784 that the important glass-house started production in the city. It was financed with a starting capital of £10,000 from George and William Penrose. The principal craftsmanship was supplied by the importing from England of John Hill and a number of men he brought with him from Worcestershire. Hill himself was from a family who operated the Coalbournhill Glass-house near Stourbridge.

The decorating of glass by cutting and grinding goes back to Roman times. The collector is, however, unlikely to come across examples earlier than Bohemian glass; the industry was established in Prague at the start of the seventeenth century. The most common way of cutting glass is by the use of abrasive wheels. The technique produces sharp, clear edges, generally easily discernible from the blunter edges of glass moulded in imitation.

## 'Nailsea' glass

Glass can be coloured with metallic oxides or it can be decorated with enamel – a process that was known by the Romans. Medieval Islamic mosque lamps ornamented with enamel-painting are treasures eagerly sought after. Lower down the scale comes 'Nailsea' glass, which is really a generic term for a type of decoration. This was originally a type of bottle glass which carried a low rate of tax and was used to make cheap articles for stalls at country fairs. It was J. R. Lucas, a Bristol bottle-maker, who founded the factory at Nailsea in Somerset in 1788. Methods of decoration included loops of white, stripes in pink and white and other tints, flecks of various colours. Some of the principal objects included walking-sticks, jugs, pipes, rolling-pins and decanters.

Objects in this class, which were once intended for the mass-market, are difficult to date. Their original wave of popularity lasted till late in the nineteenth century, but during the last few years there has been a considerable revival of interest.

(*opposite*) Cut-glass candelabrum of the early eighteenth century

(*right*) A Nailsea carafe

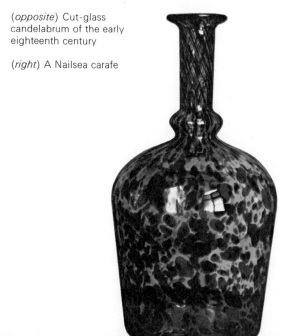

(*above*) An Art Nouveau vase from Austria; (*opposite*) A 'stick' barometer of about 1800

## 'Art Nouveau'

One of the most distinctive decorative styles of the last hundred years was the so-called 'Art Nouveau', which evolved around the 1890s and spread across America and Europe. It flourished especially in Britain and Belgium. Many of the basic patterns consist of writhing, naturalistic plant forms. The vogue swept the whole field of design from architecture to furniture, from glass to metalwork. There was an underlying intention to fuse a sense of movement into the object being treated. Some of the things are moulded to suggest animate forms. Grueby Faience Company in Boston made pottery vases simulating folded petals; Tiffany of America produced glass like lilies. The glass has a frosty surface often with runny mixed colours.

The Arts and Crafts Movement of William Morris in England may have been the basic inspiration behind 'Art Nouveau'. This earlier Movement was to all intents and purposes a protest against the rising tide of mass-production.

# Scientific instruments

The technological age of today has led to a great increase in the interest of acquiring examples of early scientific instruments. Under the heading of astronomy can come astrolabes, orreries and quadrants. For the mathematician there are early calculating instruments, such as sectors and Napier's bones. There are the sights, levels and shot calipers employed by the old gunners.

One of the most specialized fields is that of the clock and watch collector. Here it is a must to have at least an outline knowledge of the various types of clocks and watches and their movements, and more than this, to be at the ready to detect 'marriages', particularly with long-case clocks, where faces and movements may have been switched.

Barometers can range from the early cistern types – where the tube is placed below the level of mercury in an open reservoir – to the aneroid. There is the wheel barometer that uses a 'J' tube and has on top of the mercury a small float connected by a thread to a pointer, which allows for an accurate reading on a scale.

## Carpets and rugs

Carpets and rugs had their origin in the East. When they were introduced into Europe during the fifteenth and sixteenth centuries they were used at first as coverings for tables, chests and beds, whilst the floors were spread with rushes, straw or sand. Foot-carpets were a mark of rank, being reserved for kings and nobles.

The carpet industry in Europe was first developed in France where a factory was established at the Louvre in 1608 by Henry IV. In 1685, when the Edict of Nantes was revoked, many of the weavers, who were mostly Protestant, fled across the channel and brought the industry to England. The Flemish weavers first settled in Bristol and from there the craft soon spread to other centres including Kidderminster, Dewsbury and Glasgow.

A study of portraits and interior scenes painted in the sixteenth and seventeenth centuries can provide much information regarding the early designs for carpets and rugs, their colours and also their use.

To a degree, the fineness of the work can govern the value of specimens, ranging from the finest carpets from Bokhara and Kashan with about 200 and 250 knots to the square inch respectively, to the lesser 'Turkeys' dropping to around 20 knots.

## Pottery and porcelain

One of the most famous centres for European ceramics has been the Meissen factory. It was established by Augustus II, King of Poland and Elector of Saxony, for the manufacture of hard-paste or 'true' porcelain. Here the experiments of Tschirnhausen and Böttger began in about 1706. It is to the latter that the invention of hard-paste porcelain is attributed. In 1708 Tschirnhausen died and shortly after Böttger succeeded in discovering the way of making white porcelain — it is said by the accidental detection of the necessary kaolin. The story is quoted that John Schnorr, a rich ironmaster of the Erzgebirge, in 1711, riding on horseback at Aue, near Schneeberg, observed that his horse's feet stuck continually into a soft white clay which impeded his progress.

Today pieces of Meissen, particularly small modelled groups, are amongst the most sought-after items in the saleroom.

(*opposite*) Very rare Ottoman Egyptian prayer rug; (*below*) An eighteenth-century celestial globe made of Meissen porcelain

(*left*) A Sèvres covered cup

(*opposite*) An eighteenth-
century Wedgwood salt-cellar
of black basalte

In France one of the main centres has been Sèvres. The
history of this famous factory must be traced back to that
of St Cloud, where work began as early as 1695, and which
should be considered as the parent of all the porcelain
manufactories of France. In 1735 the secret of the methods
was carried by some of the workmen to Chantilly, and works
were commenced there by the brothers Dubois. They sub-
sequently left and took the secret with them to Vincennes,
where a laboratory was given them, but after three years
they were dismissed in 1741 and replaced by their former
workman, François Cravant. In 1745 a company was set up
in the name of Charles Adam. This received official recogni-
tion from the King and was granted a special licence for the
making of porcelain.

The Charles Adam Company failed to make a profit, and in
1753 the licence was transferred exclusively to Eloy Brichard.
From then on the two interlaced 'L's became the mark for
Sèvres. It was also decided to take the factory to the village
of Sèvres. The new buildings took some time and it was not
until the end of 1756 that the factory started production.

The name of Wedgwood has become so famous that it has passed into the dictionary as a type of stoneware. It was Josiah Wedgwood, who lived between 1730 and 1795, and who was put to work at the age of ten, who was to become England's most famous potter. He combined the qualities of successful businessman, organizer and supreme technician.

By 1775 Wedgwood had perfected a ceramic body which enabled him to imitate the cameos of Antiquity, producing a fine-grained stoneware that was capable of accepting colour from a number of different metallic stains. It was then possible to apply varying types of decoration to the stoneware with a material of another colour. One of the best-known examples of 'jasper' ware is where the ground is light-blue and the applied ornament and figures are white.

The Wedgwood Works produced a very large number of cameos, medallions and vases, using this technique. Much of the success of these products was due in no small way to the skill of artists like John Flaxman, who worked for Wedgwood from 1775 to 1787.

(*above*) Chelsea. *The Grape-gatherer* and (*right*) Meissen.
*The Court Jesters Fröhlich and Schmiedel.* (*opposite*) Pewter jug
with side handle

Another of the well-known centres in England has been
Chelsea. The works were established in or about the year
1745, and some of the labour force was recruited from Bow,
Burslem and other places. Two of the prime movers were
Charles Gouyn, a jeweller, and Nicholas Sprimont, a silversmith. The similarity of some of the early Chelsea work to
that of St Cloud may have been that for a time a French
chemist worked in Chelsea. There are four main periods for
the Chelsea factory under the aegis of Sprimont: 1745–9
(triangle); 1749–52 (raised anchor); 1753–7 (red anchor);
1758–69 (gold anchor).

Louis François Roubillac, the French sculptor – who
created the monument to Handel in Westminster Abbey and
the statue of Shakespeare in the British Museum – was one of
the artists who modelled for Sprimont. A number of the most
important groups and figures produced at the Chelsea
factory are attributed to him.

# Pewter

Pewter is an alloy of tin with varying proportions of lead. The name is thought to have been derived from 'spelter' which was used with local alliteration by other European countries; with the Dutch it was 'peauter'; with the French 'peutre'; with the Italians 'peltro'. The oldest known pewter is of Roman times and it had a composition of about 71 per cent tin with 28 per cent lead, the remainder being a fraction of iron, which may have been accidental.

A thousand or more years later the pewter-makers of Montpelier used a recipe with 96 per cent tin. Craftsmen at Limoges made up their pewter using four parts of lead to one hundred parts of tin. There was an early English secret formula that specified the adding of a small amount of brass to give the pewter greater strength.

Pewter first appears in history in 1074, when a synod at Rouen allowed it to be used as a substitute for gold or silver in church vessels. The records of its domestic use start in about 1274, when pewter cauldrons were used for boiling the meat at the coronation of Edward I.

English pewter, broadly speaking, is much less ornate than that of the Continent of Europe. A wide variety of objects have been made from the alloy, including plates, tankards, ink-stands, snuff-boxes, candle-sticks and salt-cellars.

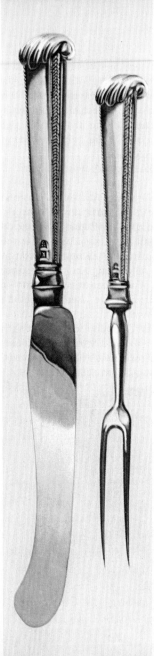

## Cutlery

Although fine-quality eating knives were produced in England during the Middle Ages, very few have survived. The high-quality English knife of the latter part of the sixteenth century often had a handle which was built up of layers of amber, bone, ebony and ivory, separated by brass washers. The hallmark books of both the Sheffield and the London Cutlers' Company record the names and marks of many seventeenth-century cutlers. Many of the examples of work that can still be seen are by a few London craftsmen, including William Lambert and Hans Smyth.

Forks for eating at table were not known in England until towards the end of the reign of Queen Elizabeth I. Those that did appear were brought back by travellers from Italy. It is recorded that in 1581 the Countess of Lincoln presented the Queen with a fork, knife and spoon of crystal, ornamented with gold and set with 'sparks of garnets'. Early forks had two prongs, the three-pronged type coming later, and the four-pronged not coming into general use until the end of the eighteenth century.

The earliest known English-made silver fork bears the London hallmark for 1632–3.

## Silver

Silver next to gold is the most malleable and ductile of metals. From early times vessels and other items have been made from it for devotional and luxury purposes. The Assyrians, Egyptians, Greeks, Phœnicians and Romans worked in silver. Pliny mentions suppers served on pure and antique silver and Horace refers to Roman homes gleaming with silver.

In former days the chief sources of supply were Hungary, Transylvania and Spain. Since the discovery of America, large quantities have come particularly from Mexico and Peru. To give some idea of the amounts used about a hundred years ago, the total world production was close on 4,000 tons.

The silversmith's art, as with that of the goldsmith, is closely related to the work of the jeweller, the enameller, the sculptor and the engraver. Besides this, he must be adept at metalwork techniques including annealing, casting, hammerwork and soldering. And, as often as not, he must be an accomplished designer.

Apart from the aesthetic attraction of silver, it also has the

(*opposite*) George III silver 'pistol grip' knife and fork; (*right*) Silver perfume burner with the hallmark for 1628

advantage, with eating-vessels, in that it is resistant to many acids and alkalis. A disadvantage in our often heavily polluted environment is that it can very quickly become tarnished.

Some of the most important ways of decorating silver include chasing, engraving, piercing, *repoussé* and *niello*. Chasing is the art of producing ornament by the use of steel implements. The tools, when struck with a hammer, do not gouge out the metal, but shift it to form the pattern. The technique calls for considerable skill to achieve an even effect. Very delicate results may be attained; as for example, the watch-cases by G. M. Moser (1704–83). The earliest work that was pierced had the decoration made by using a hammer and chisel. It was towards the end of the eighteenth century that a piercing-saw was introduced. *Repoussé* is a form of chasing, where all the punching is done from the back. To protect the design whilst it is made, the piece is held against a soft bed that may be of wax or wood. *Niello* work dates from Roman times. With this method the engraved design is filled with an amalgam of silver, copper and lead, which is mixed with sulphur. When this amalgam is fused it turns black.

One of the most popular collectors' pieces is the coffee pot. Coffee houses were first known in Cairo, and were established in Constantinople in the latter part of the sixteenth century. By the second half of the seventeenth century they had been set up in many European cities, including Nuremberg (1686), Hamburg (1679) and Marseilles (1671). The first coffee house in London seems to have been opened in St Michael's Alley, Cornhill, in 1652.

Chocolate was introduced at almost the same time as coffee, and, broadly speaking, the shapes and the designs for the two pots progressed together, the main exception being that chocolate pots had some form of aperture in the lid to allow for the insertion of a stirring-instrument. The chocolate that was drunk then was not the thin liquid we know today. It generally had considerable sediment and was a thickish liquid owing to the high percentage of cocoa fat. It was not until the 1820s, when Van Houten discovered a process to extract more of this fat, that the drink became thinner.

(*opposite*) A magnificent inkstand of 1639 with *repoussé* decoration and cast figures ; (*right*) Eighteenth-century coffee pot with chased and engraved decoration

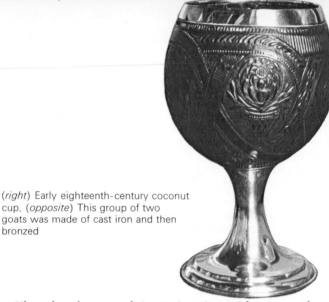

(*right*) Early eighteenth-century coconut cup. (*opposite*) This group of two goats was made of cast iron and then bronzed

Silver has been used in conjunction with many other materials. A popular item was, and is, the coconut cup. There are examples dating back to late Medieval times. The nut, being very hard, will take a high polish, and the dark rich colour contrasts pleasingly with delicate silverwork. One curiosity of the sixteenth century was the passion for mounting ostrich eggs. These, not altogether beautiful objects, were prized for their rarity and have been mounted with great skill and considerable decoration. The highly worked silver appears to contrast rather strangely with the somewhat crude spotted egg.

Mother-of-pearl has been used, as has the nautilus shell. The nautilus comes from the Indo-Pacific Ocean and the external part of the shell can be brown in colour and marked by dark bands, 'like a tortoiseshell cat'. Ceramic pots and glassware have also been enhanced by the silversmith's craft, as have objects of horn and ivory.

## Sculpture

Sculpture is rather a loose, generic term, under which can be grouped wood and stone carving, modelling and casting. The classic material for true sculpture is marble. The stone has a very fine texture and so lends itself to the production of a highly polished plastic surface. The Greeks were masters in its use, and from early Roman times sculptors in Italy have cut their supplies from the famous Carrara quarries. During the Renaissance, particularly in Germany and Austria, wood was one of the favourite materials, as not only did the different timbers provide variations in colour, but also in grain, which could be exploited by the carver.

The appreciation of bronze casts has a fascination of its own; for the free manipulation which is possible with soft clay is transferred into a hard, permanent material. The skilled technique of hollow casting, which is known as 'cire perdue', has been used for thousands of years. This consists in constructing a model with a wax surface of suitable thickness. This is covered with plaster and the whole heated, so that the wax melts and runs out through channels cut for the purpose. Molten bronze is then poured in to fill the vacant space.

(*right*) Fourteenth-century French ivory with scenes showing the Crowning of the Virgin and the Presentation of Christ in the Temple

(*opposite*) Silk pillow lace made in Dublin about 1856

## Ivory

The first ivory carvings appeared some 20,000 years ago, during the Aurignacian period. They were made from mammoth tusks. Since then practically all the advancing cultures of the world have worked at one form or another of this art. Strictly speaking, the word 'ivory' means the tusk of an elephant. But practically, it includes the tusks of the walrus, the hippopotamus, and other animals.

Ivory has been used a great deal for religious purposes – objects such as crucifixes, liturgical combs, the heads of pastoral staves, and even altarpieces. It has been much in favour for the decoration of palaces. The Romans sent an ivory throne to Porsena, King of Clusium, and Queen Victoria had one presented to her by an Indian Prince.

Other works of art and craft which have been made from the material include chessmen, snuff-boxes, toilet combs, mirror cases and hunting-horns.

In substance and structure ivory is really a tooth formed

out of phosphates, and similar substances, lying in layers deposited by the growth process.

## Lace

The development of lace started in the late fifteenth century. It was first made by the nuns in convents, for use on church linen and vestments. The art soon spread to the Royal Courts and became a pastime for ladies of leisure. Mary, Queen of Scots and Mary, wife of William of Orange, were both expert makers of 'points', (lace made with a needle).

Lace as an ornament to clothing and in fashion has been sought-after for centuries. It can be seen in portraits from the past, particularly those of the Dutch and Spanish schools.

Pillow lace is made by hand with bobbins on a pillow. It is believed to have been invented by Barbara Uttmann of Saint Annaberg, Saxony, in the mid-sixteenth century. But it must have been known in Flanders at an earlier date, according to a picture painted in 1495 by Quentin Matsys. In pillow lace, where an elaborate pattern is being included, up to 1,000 bobbins may be used at one time.

The European centres for fine lace include Bruges, Brussels, Genoa and Venice. In Great Britain, Honiton and Nottingham are notable centres. And in Ireland centres with the greatest reputation are Carrickmacross, Limerick and Youghal.

# Embroidery

Embroidery is one of the oldest ornamental arts, and archaeological expeditions continue to throw light on its beginnings.

In England, in the late seventeenth century, one popular technique was stump work. This had a three-dimensional form which was achieved by the use of heavy raised stitches and by padding up areas from underneath. It was used for embroidered pictures and to decorate book-bindings, caskets and mirror-frames.

One form of embroidery which is a favourite for a number of collectors is the 'sampler'. The name is derived from the Latin 'exemplar', and it is defined in the dictionary as 'pattern of work – an example'. A few samplers dating back to the reign of Queen Elizabeth I, and possibly earlier, can be found in museums and private collections. The peak period was from the late sixteenth and early seventeenth centuries.

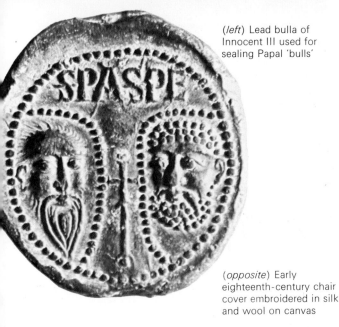

(*left*) Lead bulla of Innocent III used for sealing Papal 'bulls'

(*opposite*) Early eighteenth-century chair cover embroidered in silk and wool on canvas

## Coins and medals

Coin collecting dates back almost to the appearance of the first money. Herodotus gives the invention of stamped money to the Lydians, and the *Parian Chronicle* credits it to the Aeginetans in the ninth century BC. Among the earliest coins known are the silver examples of Aegina, which are stamped with a turtle, and the gold and silver Darics of the Persian Empire in the fifth century BC.

Throughout history the large majority of coins have been circular. This is not only for convenience, but also to prevent 'clipping' when coins were really worth their weight in gold. The designs on coins and the milled edges are also intended to prevent mutilation. Small as they are, coins can often give information from the past. Much of what we know of Greek and Roman history comes from this source.

Alongside coins, medals are generally collected; the principal difference being that the latter are struck or cast to commemorate some occasion, or person, and have no direct monetary value.

*(above)* Tenth-century wooden gaming board; *(opposite)* Two French dolls of the 1880s. The small one, with a wooden body, was made by Jumeau

## Bygones

As the more popular collectors' items become scarcer and more expensive, many people are turning towards bygones. Sometimes they are sought after because they have intimate associations with the past, confined perhaps to a single family circle or some famous person.

One of the most widespread crazes at the moment is the collecting of horse brasses. During the latter part of the nineteenth century more than three hundred different designs for brasses were being produced. Any examples being bought should be examined carefully because there is an obviously profitable trade today in the mass-production of these objects.

Toys can be traced back to very early periods. Virgil mentions the spinning-top in the seventh book of the *Aeneid* and it was probably introduced into England by the Romans. Amongst the most enthusiastic people for playing ball were the Greeks, who used three different types: the little ball, the great ball and a form of empty ball, which was probably blown up in a similar form to the modern football.

Dolls were very popular with the early Egyptians, Greeks and Romans. Primitive people all over the world had and have a delight in simple images carved out of wood or bone, modelled from clay or constructed from a mixture of materials, and to many the doll has a magical significance.

Wooden dolls came to England from the Netherlands and were first called 'Flanders babies' or, more simply, 'children's babies'. Since those early examples the manufacture and treatment of dolls has grown increasingly sophisticated, the features becoming more and more realistic. Mechanisms have allowed for the opening and shutting of eyes and movement, as well as the production of sound. The artistry and quality of the clothes has often resulted in perfect miniatures of full-sized garments.

Parallel with the care lavished on the dolls came architecture in a Lilliputian manner, with the production of dolls' houses. One of the most fantastic examples has been 'Titania's Palace', which has toured the United States, South America, Australia, New Zealand and Canada.

Growing in interest is the accumulation of film relics, early cine equipment and paraphernalia. These can range from a collection of stills, from perhaps a group of Marlene Dietrich films, to an early 35 mm cine projector labelled: *Système Demeny Breveté S.G.D.G. Elge-Paris.*

Early magic lanterns command interest whether they are of the simple paraffin burner type or the, at times, quite menacing monsters that could throw a powerful beam from an oxy-hydrogen light. To go with these are the old square glass slides that once captivated an audience as much as the television screen does today.

The early photographs by William Henry Fox Talbot are sought after not only for their rarity, but also for their own artistic quality. In this category the prints of Julia Margaret Cameron should be watched for.

Lighting appliances, particularly connected with transport, are very much in vogue, perhaps too much, because, as with horse brasses, reproduction carriage lamps are now being made in large numbers. Even the humble carbide bicycle-

(*above*) Nineteenth-century carriage lamp ; (*opposite*) *London Bridge*, oil painting by F. W. Watts

lamp, which did not disappear until the late 1930s, has become almost an object for respect, and a good pre-1914 example can be quite valuable.

## Oil paintings

A painting for some people has a magnetic quality. So wide is the field, and in some cases so quickly are prices rising, that underneath the dark cracking varnish could lie a fortune. Underneath it also can lie an almost valueless copy, or worse, an out-and-out deliberate fake. Quite apart from the faked productions of the like of Van Meegeren there is a plentiful supply of forgeries that get away with it, because they do not set out to be the work of a well-known master, but imitate, in a more humble vein, the Dutch, French or other schools. To safely avoid the pitfalls calls for long experience, and if possible, learned advice.

To collect oil paintings today requires a long purse or a perceptive eye. A field which still holds opportunity is that of the naïve painters. Here the pictures have been painted since about 1750. They would have been produced by artists who had little or no training, and the subject-matter is generally idyllic scenes, sometimes with an allegorical content; portraits with a stiff unemotional sense; and animals.

Raoul Dufy

## Water-colours and drawings

There is often some confusion between a water-colour and a gouache. True *water-colour* implies the use of transparent colours, whilst *gouache* is still of course a water-colour medium, but with this method opaque body colours are used and sometimes slight 'impasto' (thick application) treatment is brought in.

It is worthwhile sparing time to search through old folios of dog-eared sheets, as even today it is still possible to come across a good original work that has been overlooked. For many there is a special attraction with a preliminary wash drawing or water-colour sketch by an artist who intended to use it as a plan for a major finished work. Often there is a freedom and an exciting quality that is not always so evident in the final result. This can be seen especially with the works of John Constable. His first lay-ins for a subject have a broad impressionistic manner, that in some cases become tamed in the final version.

## Prints

The variety of printing processes offers scope for both the specialist, who may go for a particular printing technique, and the collector who is interested in general printing techniques.

## Japanese woodcuts

With the opening-up of Japan during the second half of the nineteenth century, European collectors became conscious of the fine quality of Japanese colour prints.

The centre for production was Tokyo and the best period for the collector ranges between 1750 and 1850. Prior to 1750 most of the prints were in black and white and were made primarily as illustrations for literature.

Artists who have contributed to the Japanese prowess with colour prints include Shunshō, Toyokuni, Yensen, Harunobu, Hokusai and Hiroshige. Hiroshige's *The 53 Stations of the Tōkaidō* is an outstanding series that gives, apart from other qualities, a highly sensitive representation of many districts of Japan, and also climatic and elemental changes. It is unlikely, however, that one could find a complete set outside a museum or private collection.

(*opposite*) *Sea and Boats*, gouache by Raoul Dufy ; (*below*) *View of Fuji over a River*, colour print by Hokusai

*Men Bathing,* engraving by Dürer

## Early prints

The first important European print-maker was the German, Martin Schongauer (c. 1430–91), who worked at Colmar. Under his leadership artists learnt to introduce subtleties of tone that gave a totally new dimension to that of the earlier works, which appeared as line productions. After Schongauer came Albrecht Dürer (1471–1528), who in his life-time produced an amazing number of prints, carried out mainly on the wood block or as metal engravings. About six etchings only have been credited to him. Dürer, either working on his own or directing professional craftsmen, developed a flawless technique that was so rich in modelling, tone control and hatching, that with just black and white he seemed to be able almost to suggest other colours. To examine prints by Dürer, as for example *The Knight, Death and the Devil,* is to understand how much progress with his medium he made.

## Etchings

Etching has been a medium which has attracted a large number of artists, as it has an intimacy that can be watched over during the whole process. Principally it has been carried out using either a copper or a zinc plate.

The process is briefly that the plate is heated and a ground, which is a mixture of resins, asphaltum and wax, is applied. The artist may then transfer his design with some light lines of paint, or more generally work directly using a needle to cut away the ground and expose the metal. An acid resistant varnish is then applied to the back of the plate and the whole is then lowered into a bath of nitric acid or mordant. The usual rule is to carry out the etching in several states. This means that after a preliminary needling has been done the plate is placed in the acid for a short time, then removed and the ground wiped off, so that the progress of the work can be judged. The plate can then be regrounded and the use of the needle continued. The printing of an etching is made in a reverse manner to the relief print, in that the ink is forced into the etched lines and the surface of the plate wiped.

*The Return of the Prodigal Son,* etching by Rembrandt

## Woodcuts and wood engravings

Woodcutting and wood engraving had a return to popularity in the early part of this century, particularly with the German artists associated with the *Die Brücke* Movement. Practitioners such as Karl Schmidt-Rottluff and Ernst Ludwig Kirchner have brought a vigorous manner to the woodcut, which, to a degree, had been lost since the earlier periods.

A woodcut is carried out using the plank or long grain of the wood which can be box, cherry, apple or any other hard timbers. A wood engraving is made using the end-grain which being much denser allows for fine detail. The woods used in both cases can be the same, although box, particularly that which is known as Turkish, is the favourite for wood engraving. Both methods call for skill and concentration in the cutting, for if a mistake is made, it is nearly impossible to correct.

A box block, which becomes even harder with printing, can allow for a very large run of prints indeed. The printing is relief, the opposite from intaglio – as with etching – the ink being rolled or dabbed on to the wood that has been left untouched by the *graver* or *burin*.

# LOOKING AFTER ANTIQUES

## Woodworm

The four most common types of wood-boring insects are: the common furniture beetle, the death-watch beetle, the powder-post beetle and the house longhorn beetle. The life cycle of the beetle is not necessarily one year; the larvae can remain hidden in the wood sometimes for several years. It is not the beetle that does the damage; it is the larvae or grubs.

The female beetles will normally lay their eggs in old joints or cracks and are encouraged to do so where there has been an accumulation of dust and grime. If dirt is not allowed to gather, to a degree this menace is discouraged. The beetle generally prefers timber which is fifteen years old, or more. A favourite is plywood which has been bonded with animal glue, and which often may have been put in as a backing for a mirror, a picture-frame, or a drawer. Where possible, if found, this particular material should be replaced or given very careful treatment.

The spring or early summer is the time to keep alert, as it is then that the beetle will hatch out, and its places of exit can be noted by tiny piles of powdered wood.

(*opposite*) Twentieth-century woodcut; (*below*) Signs of woodworm in a chair

Treating a chair leg with anti-woodworm fluid

Treatment for woodworm should be undertaken at the very first sign of infestation. It cannot be emphasized enough how important it is, that a regular inspection of furniture and timber of the house should be made. If the infestation is at all serious or the piece in question valuable, expert advice should be sought and professionals should be called in to carry out a full treatment. There are companies who will undertake this work and generally guarantee a period of protection.

Where it is a matter of a single piece of furniture, it can quite simply be treated in the home. An anti-woodworm fluid can be used, either with a container which has a fine nozzle, or better still, an aerosol. The latter has the advantage that it can pump out the liquid with greater pressure and so penetrate deeper into the wood. It is important when doing this that the eyes should be protected, as the poisonous liquid can often spurt out of a woodworm hole, sometimes quite a distance away from the one that is being injected. Go very thoroughly over the infected piece to make sure that all the holes are treated. For added protection after treatment, a wax furniture polish which contains anti-woodworm ingredients should be used.

In certain cases the multi-borings of the beetles may have reduced the solid wood almost to a honeycomb. Walnut is particularly liable to heavy attack. Today there are treatments available using synthetic resins and bonding agents that can penetrate the damaged timber and renew the strength. If the piece is of no great value an experiment can be carried out in the home. Turn the piece so that the worst bored part is uppermost and then with some moist clay, or other plastic substance, put a collar round the leg or arm, or whatever part is being treated, to seal off the holes. A synthetic resin glue can be mixed to a rather more liquid consistency than if being used normally. This should next be poured slowly on to the top of the part being treated, so that it will soak down into the holes. Patience is required, as it may take quite a time for thorough penetration. It is important that plenty of glue is used and that it should be allowed to set for the best part of a week before the clay, or other material, is removed.

Applying a wax polish to treated furniture

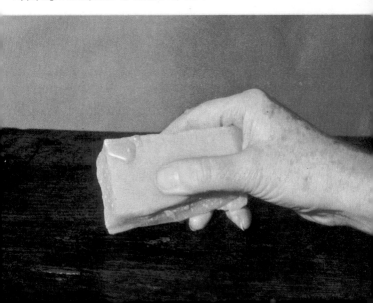

Using cleaning fluid on the back of a newly acquired chair

## Furniture

It is very important that grime is removed from furniture before polishing. Solid or liquid polishes by themselves are unlikely to remove this disfigurement and at worst may even fix it so that it will be difficult to get off later. The deposits will depend on the district but they can easily include pollutants from the air which may be greasy or tarry. Proprietary furniture cleaners can be purchased, but it is quite simple to make up one of your own and incidentally much cheaper (see recipe at end of book).

Furniture, as with many works of art and craft, has often been subjected to a number of indignities in the past. With wood these can include a mistaken treatment with clear or coloured varnishes, or French polish which may have been applied to cover blemishes. If the object has no great value, a commercial paint stripper can be applied carefully, either with a brush or a piece of cotton wool. Rubber gloves should be worn to protect the hands. After treatment the area must be sluiced with turpentine substitute (white spirit) to remove the stripper together with the dissolved polish or varnish.

Small holes such as defunct woodworm borings, cracks and scratches are best filled. This is not only from an aesthetic point of view, but it also prevents the accretion of grime. This can be done with so-called 'plastic wood' which can be bought at the local hardware store. A similar material can be made up quite easily using a fine sawdust mixed with some synthetic glue to a paste. The advantage of making it yourself is that you can add dry pigments to tint it so that it matches the wood. When using this, or the bought variety, the hole should be filled slightly 'proud' as the material will shrink.

For small scratches, that may have been caused by heavy or sharp edges, a beeswax stick can be used; if the wax is melted, a dry pigment can be added to get the right colour. In America hardware or paint shops can be found that have sets of wax sticks in different colours. For a very fine scratch the damage can sometimes be rectified by the gentle application of a lump of carnauba wax. It is to be emphasized that this wax is very hard and the application should be more in the way of a caress than with forceful rubbing.

Treating ring marks on a table

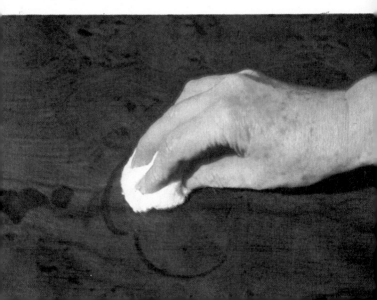

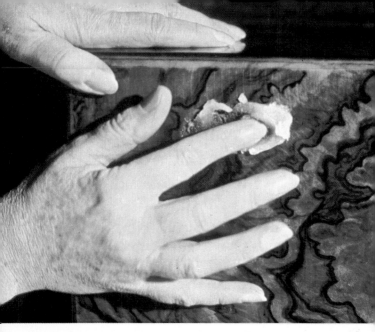

Polishing the surface of a box with home-made polish

One of the most prevalent damages to the top surface of tables, bureaux or commodes is that from a liquid. This can be from the over-filling of a flower vase or from a spilt drink. Very quickly an unsightly blemish can develop. If the stain is on a veneered surface it may cause a lifting of the veneer. Treatment should be given as soon as possible or the defect can be almost impossible to remove. In the first instance teak oil can be tried which should be quite liberally applied and left on for several hours. The residue should then be wiped off and the area repolished.

If the foregoing will not work, an application can be made of a mixture of linseed oil and turpentine (see recipe section). With a bad stain a swab of cotton wool soaked in the liquid can be left over the area all night. It can then be removed and the residue wiped away before repolishing.

Strong sunlight should never be allowed to play upon a valuable piece of furniture for any length of time, as it will tend to bleach the colours and also dry out the woods. With this type of damage, teak oil can often do much to rectify the condition.

The exquisite patina that is achieved on antique wood surfaces is often the result of years of loving care and correct treatment. Sadly, however, it can be speedily spoilt by rash, ignorant or careless handling. It is of first importance that the piece should always be thoroughly dusted before applying any polish.

Where the piece of furniture is veneered or has inlays, it should be examined carefully to see whether parts of the veneer are lifting or pieces of inlay have come loose. If the veneer lifts are serious, the wisest course is to employ a competent furniture restorer. Small pieces of loose inlay can be refixed using either a water-soluble glue such as hoof or rabbit-skin or a clear synthetic glue in a tube. Whichever adhesive is used, it should be applied sparingly and any excess should be wiped away from the top surface at once. The area should then be left to set for twenty-four hours with some form of heavy weight to hold it down.

Making up the polish

Using a card shield to protect woodwork from metal polish

A good polish is one that will produce and perpetuate the sheen of age and at the same time will not be easily marked by finger prints. A number of waxes of synthetic and natural origin have been and are made up into polishes, but so far there is nothing to equal beeswax. There are proprietary brands that contain a high percentage of this, but it is very easy to make up your own beeswax polish (see recipes at the end). Broadly speaking, the polish for solid wood furniture can be fairly stiff, but for veneers and inlays it should have more the consistency of a soft paste or cream, as this will be less likely to rupture the sometimes delicate surfaces. Polish, of whatever type, should always be applied sparingly, and then if possible left for about half an hour before being buffed up with a soft cloth. If it is applied too generously, the result is likely to be a smeary, unsatisfactory finish that is liable to catch and hold dust. The use of a revolving electrical polisher is not recommended, as it can leave a series of unsightly circular marks.

The treatment of a piece of furniture which is made of other materials, besides wood, should be approached with care. Ormolu, in particular, needs specialized handling. This is quite often lacquered to avoid tarnish and the lacquer may break down and stains of tarnish appear. Ormolu castings may have been gilded, and if there is any doubt, expert advice should be sought before treating. The lacquer, which may be of a shellac or cellulose base, will first have to be removed. This can be done by trial attempts with alcohol or acetone. As far as possible the woodwork round the ormolu mounting should be shielded. Once the lacquer is off, the ormolu can be gently scrubbed with a soft brush dipped into a solution of soap and water with a little ammonia added. If the tarnishing is obstinate, the strength of the ammonia can be increased. After the treatment the piece should be rinsed carefully, dried, and then, if desired, relacquered. Wherever possible the ormolu mount should be unscrewed, as this will obviate damage to the wood.

Another protective shield

Cracks in an antique table resulting from central heating

When polishing brass or other handles the wood should always be protected, as metal polishes can very easily attack the patina. Polish can also get into cracks and when it dries out leaves unsightly white marks.

Ivory decorated keyholes can be cleaned with reasonable safety using the minimum of water with a mild detergent. One of the best ways of applying this is to use a small piece of cotton wool wrapped round the end of an orange-stick. Immediately afterwards the areas should be rinsed, again with the minimum of liquid, and then thoroughly dried.

If it is desired to bleach the ivory or bone, a stiff paste can be made up of whiting (chalk) mixed with weak hydrogen peroxide. The paste should be applied to the area with a brush or palette-knife and left on in the first instance for about five minutes. It should then be removed and progress noted. If necessary the strength of the hydrogen peroxide should then be increased and a second application made. Finally, careful rinsing with damp swabs of cotton wool should remove all traces of the paste.

## Central heating and air-conditioning

Central heating, which may provide comfort, can be a menace, if not watched, particularly to furniture. Even worse can be the effects of air-conditioning. With both of these the danger can come not only from change of temperature, but more so from changes in the relative humidity. They tend to dry the air, so that a combination of warmth with a low humidity is produced, and this is likely to crack woodwork, even if under earlier conditions it may have remained perfect for centuries.

One remedy is to bring on the heating system slowly with the advent of the colder weather. Allow the desired temperature to build up over at least a week. Secondly, a humidifier can be used which will help to stabilize the humidity. This can be a simple water-container hanging on a radiator, or a more sophisticated free-standing appliance. An instrument called a *hygrometer* will register humidity – a reading of between 50 and 65 per cent. is desirable.

You should also watch localized sources of heat, such as electric radiators, gas or oil stoves, and see that they are not placed so as to play directly on to a piece of furniture. At the same time inspect for cold draughts that can come through loosely fitting doors or windows.

Restoring a horse's leather boot with a home-made preservative

Regluing the leather binding on an old book

## Leather

Leather is liable to attack from beetles and moths. It is particularly prone to damage from damp, which will bring on disfiguring moulds and it will be affected by strong sunlight. Furthermore, if the atmosphere is excessively dry, it will quickly deteriorate and crack.

There are a number of leather preservatives that can be bought, but one of the best can be made up in the home (see recipe at end). When using this preparation it must be remembered, that it is extremely inflammable and fire precautions must be taken. The bottle should be shaken thoroughly and the liquid applied with a piece of cotton wool and gently rubbed into the surface, and then left for twenty-four hours. At the end of that time the excess can be wiped off and the surface polished. This dressing can often perform miracles and will not only bring back the 'body' to the leather, but also will bring up the colour.

If the leather is very dirty it can be washed gently using the minimum of warm water with pure soap and applying it with a soft brush, rinsing with damp cotton wool. This should never, however, be done if there are any signs of splitting or peeling in the leather. Grime may also be removed by the application of turpentine, but it is wise to make a test in a very small area that as far as possible is not noticeable; this way you can make sure that any colours present will not be removed.

Unfortunately one often comes across examples of leather that have been varnished to improve the appearance. This is a course that should not be followed, as leather can swell or contract with alterations in temperature and humidity and the varnish film will soon crack and become disfigured.

Where leather coverings on a desk-top or a table have started to come away, they should be refixed as soon as possible. Using a scalpel or small knife, the old adhesive should be carefully scraped away from the mounting-wood and the leather. The new glue may be either hoof or rabbit-skin, or better still, a synthetic resin emulsion containing a plasticizer, which will allow it to move with the leather. Use as little adhesive as possible and ease the lifted leather back into place, leaving it to set under a weight.

Stains can be removed from leather with an electric iron and blotting paper

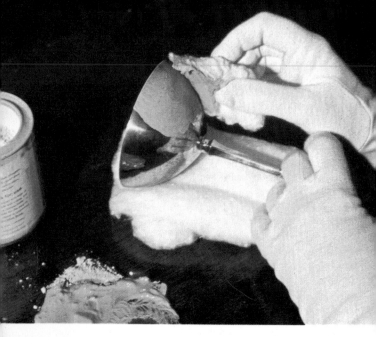

Cleaning silver with a proprietary polish

Wax and grease stains can, to a large extent, be removed from leather by heat. With candlewax the excess should first be carefully scraped off with a small blunt knife. The best heat source is from a thermostatically controlled household iron. It should be set at the lowest temperature, which is generally for silk. Two or three thicknesses of white blotting paper, or failing that, clean brown paper should be placed over the stains and the iron applied with gentle pressure. Leave on for a few seconds and then examine the progress. Repeat with a clean area of the paper until no more wax or grease can be removed.

The treatment of ink or wine stains on leather can be unpredictable, and if the piece is of value, an expert should be consulted. However, if the specimen has no great value and the stains are small, some improvement can be achieved by judicious use of white spirit or soap and water, in both cases applied sparingly and the operation watched carefully.

## Metalwork
### Silver

The cleaning of silver causes some argument as to which is the safest and most efficient method. The traditional way has been the use of powders mixed to a paste with water or alcohol. More recently introduced is the electrochemical method.

As with furniture polishes, so with silver cleaners. Almost every year, new brands and types appear in the stores. The principal point to remember is that silver is incredibly easy to scratch, and once this has happened it can be very difficult – and sometimes nearly impossible – to restore the exquisite sheen that is one of the main attractions of the metal. Any of the plate powders or pastes used should be very fine and smooth. If rubbed between the fingers there should be no feeling of grit or roughness. Most of the proprietary brands are safe and have adequate instruction, which should be followed implicitly. If using dry powders, it is possibly best to apply them mixed with methylated spirit, as this will tend to spread them more evenly and to enable the penetration of detailed work.

Before making a start at cleaning a silver object it is a good plan to use a magnifying glass to examine it. This should

Electrochemical cleaning of silver like this is non-abrasive

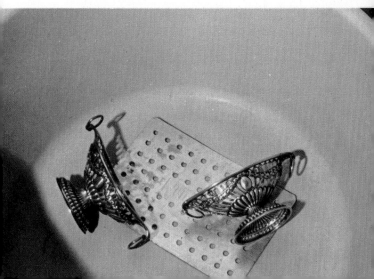

Electrochemical cleaning with a cotton wool swab. Note the rubber gloves

allow you to pick up minute marks running in the same direction, which will have been made by the maker when he applied the first polish. The general direction of these marks should be followed when cleaning with powders or pastes. Soft cotton gloves should be worn, as even a piece of hard skin on the fingers or a finger-nail can quickly cause a blemish. Rings also are possible sources of damage.

To some extent the electrochemical methods of cleaning are the safest, because with these there is no question of abrasion. The proprietary liquid brands should be used exactly as the instructions say. One very important point is that a container of the liquid should be used for only one metal.

One of the simplest ways of cleaning in the electrochemical method is to put a piece of aluminium sheet or crumpled aluminium foil in a large bowl. Some hardware stores have pieces of perforated aluminium which are specially made for this process. Lay the pieces of silver on the aluminium, so that they all touch it. Now immerse the silver in a solution of washing-soda and hot water; the strength need not be more than about 5 per cent. The liquid will bubble and some fumes will come off, but this need not cause worry. After about a minute the pieces can be lifted out and will normally have the tarnish removed. Needless to say, strong rubber gloves or wooden tongs should be used.

By whichever method silver has been cleaned, it should be given a thorough rinsing in plenty of warm water. In general, when washing silver that will have been used for eating purposes, or when rinsing it after cleaning, a piece of foam sheet should be put at the bottom of the bowl and where possible, one piece, or at the most two or three pieces, washed at a time. Never jangle a whole mass of silver in a washing-up bowl, as this will inevitably cause scratching.

Where you have to deal with an object such as a cake basket or an epergne, which is too large to go into a proprietary container or to fit into a bowl, the electrochemical method can be carried out using swabs of cotton wool dipped in the liquid; again wearing rubber gloves. A device that can work with a very ornate object is to put it in a heavy, clear plastic bag with the silver-dip and work it around, so that the liquid reaches every part.

If intricate chasing on a large object is being treated, the polish should be applied with a piece of cotton wool wrapped round a wooden splint. Adequate cushioning should be provided on the cleaning table to prevent damage whilst the piece is being cleaned.

It must be pointed out that electrochemical cleaning should

Intricate chasing can be cleaned with cotton wool on an orange-stick

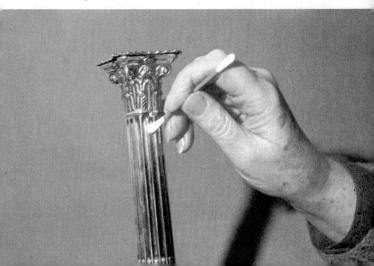

Fine silver should if possible be stored in individual flannel bags

not be used on Sheffield plate, for if any of the base metal is showing complications can occur.

For intermediary cleaning there are a number of proprietary silver cloths on the market which will remove light tarnish. If these are used, any silver that is intended for eating purposes should be rinsed and dried, as described earlier.

The storage of silver needs some care. There have been instances where carefully polished silver has been put away in a cupboard or even in a display cabinet and has unaccountably quickly tarnished. One possible reason for this is that the cupboard or cabinet may have recently been painted out. Unfortunately some household paints contain volatile sulphur impurities. When possible, the paintwork should be carried out using an oil-bound colour. Another unsuspected source of tarnish can be textiles that have been recently cleaned, as some establishments use chemicals that contain sulphur.

For display purposes silver can be lacquered. There are a number of products that can be purchased and the treatment should be as follows. The object must first be scrupulously cleaned and then as a further precaution, de-greased. This latter can be done using pieces of cotton wool dipped in methylated spirit. When this has evaporated, the lacquer should be applied using a soft brush. The trick is to apply it evenly, and the best way is to hold the piece under a strong light, so that the application can be clearly seen. If minute areas are missed, all too soon these will show up, as streaks of tarnish will appear. Normally a good lacquer will give protection for up to a year. To re-lacquer, the old lacquer must first be removed with acetone and the whole process repeated.

For the display of an especially precious piece, it is worthwhile having a special airtight case made. This should include in the base a substance, such as *silica gel*.

It is quite permissible to use a brush when cleaning elabor-

A soft hair brush can be used for cleaning decorated silver

Rust first has to be softened with paraffin

ately decorated pieces of silver. It must be emphasized, however, that this should be of soft hair, not of nylon or bristle, as the latter two can quickly scratch.

It is extremely unwise with obstinate cases of heavy tarnish to use acids or strong caustic liquids. Furthermore, never be tempted to use harsh abrasive materials, such as steel wool, or even the finest of sand-papers. Physical damage in the way of dents or bends should always be left to the skilled professional.

## Iron and steel

In a damp climate, iron and steel pieces can cause much trouble. Locks and hinges on furniture, fireguards, steel cutlery, can all too quickly show signs of deterioration in the form of a thin reddish veil of rust, which, if it is neglected, will very soon take a firm hold and be nearly impossible to remove. Ugly disfiguring pits will appear in the metal.

The first course is to soften the rust. Where possible the object should be immersed in paraffin (kerosene). Depending on the state of the attack, the piece should be left soaking for about twelve hours. With hinges or locks which are impossible to immerse, swabs of cotton wool, or lint soaked in paraffin, can be wrapped around them, taking as much care as possible to shield the surrounding wood. One method here can be to use strips of plastic adhesive tape.

After the soaking, the metal can be worked over, using small pieces of steel wool or a stiff brush, watching carefully that the method is not doing more damage than is the rust. Plate powders can also be used with pieces of cotton wool – a small area being worked over at a time. Effort must be made to keep the cleaning even, and also to avoid leaving any obvious pattern with the rubbing.

For the more obstinate cases of rust paraffin may not be found strong enough to soften the blemish. There are available, in hardware stores or garages, proprietary rust-

Working over the metal with rust remover and steel wool

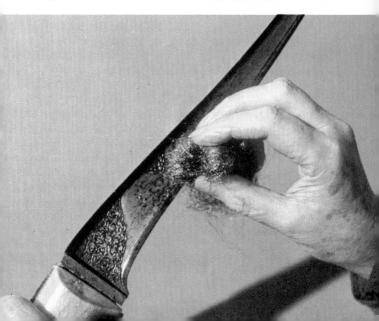

A protective coating of wax or lanolin being applied

softening preparations. These may be either in liquid or
jelly form. The best way to apply them is with a soft brush,
making repeated applications to get the full effect. Again,
follow the instructions on the container, as the different
preparations can have varying strengths. After they have
had time to work, they should be rinsed away with paraffin
and the softened rust removed with steel wool or a brush.

With weapons that have been attacked, especially with
swords that may have gold or silver damascene decoration,
the use of proprietary rust-removers is not advised. The
most that should be attempted is a soaking with paraffin,
and after that with a careful application of weak nitric acid
mixed with methylated spirit. You must wear rubber gloves,
and put on the acid and spirit with a small piece of cotton
wool. As the acid can cause etching, an application should
literally be no more than for a few seconds, and then the
object should be rinsed immediately, very thoroughly, in
clean water.

Once iron or steel objects have been cleaned, as far as
possible they should be kept in a dry atmosphere. With

many houses this is often easier said than done, particularly with old buildings that may be close to rivers and have been erected without damp-proofing precautions. Once again, our urban civilization unfortunately provides an atmosphere with too much sulphur, and this agent can accelerate rusting.

Iron and steel can be lacquered or varnished. But neither of these courses produces a satisfying aesthetic result. A better course is to use lanolin, although this can be difficult to apply. It should be put on with a finger-tip, as thinly as possible, and then wiped with a clean rag, so that a sticky surface is not left which can attract dust. Better still is to use a creamy paste prepared from beeswax and turpentine. The wax should be melted first and then removed from the heat and enough turpentine added to achieve the consistency.

## Pewter

Pewter is one of the most difficult alloys to deal with, as one must strike a happy medium. Antique pots and plates acquire a recognizable patina of their own, and as far as possible this

Examining jewellery for loose stones before cleaning

Polishing a pewter jug with a chamois leather

should be preserved. Furthermore, pewter is very soft and can quite easily be dented or deformed even by fairly gentle cleaning.

No attempt should ever be made to go to work on a pewter object with abrasive powders or to dip it into liquids with the aim of producing a gleaming finish, as one does with polished silver. There are some quite horrific household remedies that include the use of hydrochloric acid, caustic soda and even harsh scouring powders and steel wool.

A first attempt should be made using nothing more than a soft chamois or polishing-cloth. If this does not bring up the desired effect, the object can be gently washed in warm, soapy water and then thoroughly dried and re-buffed. A final course could be the application of the finest possible plate-powder, using only a minimal quantity and applying it with an oily rag.

## Brass

Brass, an alloy of copper and zinc, can normally be safely cleaned with any of the proprietary polishes that state they are intended for it. If the object is very dirty, it is best that it should first be well washed with hot water and soap and then dried before the polish is applied. In extreme cases, where tarnish and grime will not yield, harsher methods can be used. A strong solution of sodium carbonate in hot water can be prepared and the pieces lowered into it and moved about, a watch being kept during the process. Rubber gloves or tongs must be used. Another drastic method is to dissolve half an ounce of oxalic acid in a quart of water and, again wearing heavy rubber gloves, applying this solution with swabs of cotton wool to the object. After treatment the object should be rinsed throughly. Protective treatment after cleaning includes lacquering, and many housewives believe firmly in a thin application of furniture cream, which cannot do much harm and can be easily removed with methylated spirit.

Bronze should be treated with great care

## Bronze

Bronze, an alloy of copper and tin, is a totally different case from brass and is rather like pewter in that it should be treated with great respect. Often all that is required is just a gentle dusting with a soft brush.

It is essential that the patina of bronze should not be disturbed. This colouring of the metal may be the result of age, or a combination of the artist's intent and the result of time. It may range in colour from near-black to dark-brown and range from grey-blue greens to a gleaming golden yellow when the cast has been polished.

A careless minute with an abrasive polish will not only spoil the aesthetic effect of a bronze figure, but can seriously drop the value of the piece. The soundest advice for an un-polished bronze cast that has patination is to do no more than carefully dust. But with a polished cast, showing a golden yellow colour, a very discreet use of a high quality brass polish may be made. As with silver, it is vital that the cloths are spotlessly clean, for any gritty dust particles will soon scratch the surface.

(*left*) An unprotected bronze statue exposed to the weather; (*opposite*) Bronze Age mirror showing signs of bronze disease

A bronze statue that is standing outside braving the weather can be given some protective treatment. Industrial fumes and salt air from the seaside can attack this alloy. Before any treatment, the figure should be well cleaned with warm water and weak soap and then thoroughly dried. A paste of beeswax – as was suggested for the protection of iron and steel – should be prepared and can be wiped on to the statue; where there are complicated details, a soft brush should be used.

Ancient bronze objects are liable to exhibit a strange phenomenon called 'bronze disease'. This may also occur with more modern pieces where there has been neglect or where they have been exposed to extreme climatic conditions. The disease can first be detected when small, light blue or green spots or pimples appear on the surface. The spots, which are powdery or pastel-like according to the humidity, grow as a result of oxygen acting on cuprous chloride and changing it into basic cupric chloride. It is often thought that the main factor in bringing on 'bronze disease' is the presence of excess damp, but this is not correct. High humidity is only an assisting feature.

Some coins may be cleaned in a nitric acid bath

## Coins and medals

Extreme care is necessary when dealing with coins and medals, as any depreciation from 'mint' condition is frowned upon by the specialist collector. Silver coins, in particular, call for gentle treatment.

However, it is normally safe to cleanse bronze, copper or silver coins and medals by immersing them for a few seconds in a bath containing 5 per cent nitric acid. The coin should be picked up with some form of acid-resistant tweezers and lowered into the acid. Generally the action is almost immediate, and the coin should then be removed and well rinsed. If it is still tarnished, then before continuing the acid treatment, a strong magnifying-glass should be used to note if the metal is being etched.

Sometimes with ancient coins there may be deposits of limestone or other substances clinging to the surface. In this case, any visible areas of the metal should first be covered with beeswax, or a heavy grease, and then the acid bath treatment can be given with close scrutiny of the results. The surface of the metal may be lacquered, or treated with lanolin or beeswax paste.

## Jewellery

With jewellery, much of the grime is an accumulation of perspiration and dirt. Before a start is made on any piece, however simple, it should be examined thoroughly with a strong magnifying-glass to make quite sure that none of the stones or parts are loose. If this condition is evident, treatment is much better left to your jeweller.

Where pieces are mechanically set and there is no sign of adhesives, rings, brooches and the like can generally be quite safely washed in warm water, the process being assisted by a judicious use of a small soft-hair paintbrush. If there are still small particles of grime left, these can be gently worked over, again with a paintbrush, using methylated spirit. There are proprietary dip liquids in the stores for cleaning jewellery, and normally they will be safe if the instructions are followed carefully.

The cleaning of necklaces can be awkward, as any application of water can cause the thread to shrink. Dirty or discoloured pearls can be treated with powdered magnesia. The pearls should be placed in a small container with an adequate amount of the substance and then shaken gently for a few minutes and left in the powder overnight. They can then be removed the next day and dusted off.

Fabric dust filter on an old clock

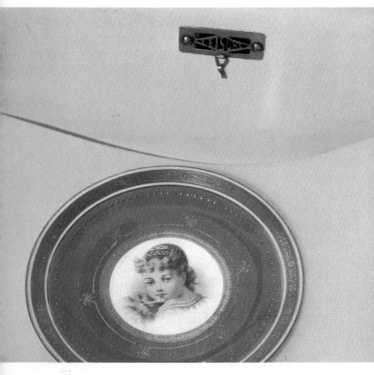

Protecting a plate with a sheet of foam plastic during washing

## Clocks

The mechanism of clocks can be complicated and sensitive and very quickly damaged by inexpert methods.

The works of many longcase (grandfather) and other large clocks can easily become affected by dust. With some wooden case clocks there may be openwork fret panels behind, which are pieces of closely woven fabric that can act as a dust filter. If these have come loose they should be refixed, or if rotten, be replaced. Where possible, open cracks in backing boards should be sealed with paper attached from the inside.

If you have an old kitchen clock – or other specimen of no great value – and it appears to have stopped just from an over-accumulation of dust, it may be immersed in a bath of petrol. This should obviously be done outside the house and certainly well away from any heat source. The works of the clock should be repeatedly lowered into the petrol and moved about to allow the liquid to wash away the grime. They should then be removed and when the petrol has evaporated the principal moving parts can be given tiny touches of light lubricating oil, applied with a brush or a feather. Too much oil is worse than none at all, for it will thicken with time, become sticky and only collect more dirt.

## Ceramics

### Cleaning

The washing of ceramics, if they are of any value, should be done with all precautions possible. The best bowl to use is a soft plastic one, and further protection can be given by placing a sheet of foam at the bottom. Rubber collars on the protruding taps are another safeguard. If a plate-drainer is used, it should be either of wooden dowel rods or a metal one that has been coated with soft plastic. The water should never be hotter than can be borne by the hands. In many cases hot water alone is sufficient, but if there are undue accretions of grease and grime, a few drops of gentle detergent may be added. After washing, the pieces should be thoroughly rinsed. Before washing, needless to say, any special pieces should be carefully inspected, and if there are any minor damages, or apparently fragile surfaces, they should be cleansed separately; this can be done, not by immersion, but with pieces of moistened cotton wool.

Coffee-pots and teapots, also cups and saucers, frequently become stained after continuous use, and for aesthetic as well as hygienic reasons stains should be removed. A word of warning however: some of the eighteenth-century glazes can be unstable, and if in doubt, advice should be sought.

Old glues often stained soft wares

For a sound piece hydrogen peroxide can be used. You should start by using a weak solution of about 5 per cent and work up to a greater strength if it is needed. Bicarbonate of soda or common salt, dissolved in water, will also assist in the removal of such stains.

Stains in cracks and also round the ring marks of saucers can be obstinate. With these, a piece of cotton wool can be saturated in the hydrogen peroxide solution and laid over the marks. It can be left on in the first instance for about ten minutes and the progress noted. If the china is pure white, and the stain very obstinate, the swabs can remain in position overnight, or even longer. Lastly, thoroughly rinse.

## Repairing ceramics
Many pieces of china will have been mended in the past, sometimes with unsightly clips, and very often with an adhesive that will have darkened, turning the hair-line joins

into ugly black lines. These old glues were generally based on animal substances such as hoof, horn or skin, also fish membranes. Although they may have stuck well, they are affected by damp and with some soft wares can cause staining. Another favourite with porcelain repairers of the nineteenth century was shellac. This again will darken.

Today there is a comparatively wide range of synthetic adhesives that can be purchased in the stores. There are two points to watch for if you are attempting home repairs. One is that the adhesive should be comparatively thin, because if it is thick it will be difficult to achieve a hair-line. The second is whether or not the adhesive can be reversed; in other words, if a join mis-sets, whether a solvent can be applied that will undo the mistake.

Epoxy glues are of a synthetic resin base and are produced in many countries. They are sold in pairs of tubes, one holding the resin, and the other a hardener. To use them, the required amounts, as mentioned in the instructions, should

Re-repairing a piece begins with dissolving the old glue

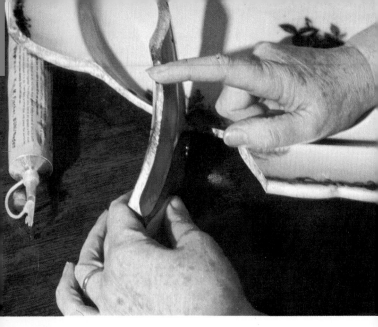

Applying new glue

be squeezed out on to a small piece of glass and the two mixed together with some form of spatula. It must be remembered that these adhesives will take some considerable time to set thoroughly. Total strength may not be achieved for several days. Gentle warmth, however, will speed up the process. The beginner may find a disadvantage with an epoxy glue in that when once it has fully set, it is practically impossible to dissolve it. Therefore it might be better to use one of the water-clear synthetic adhesives which come in a single tube and do not need a hardener.

If you are setting about to re-repair an old damaged piece, it should first be dismantled. In many cases this can be done by leaving the china standing for a period in hot water. If, however, the previous mends have not been made with animal or fish glues, solvents may have to be used. This can call for experiment. Swabs of cotton wool soaked in acetone will generally remove the early synthetic glues. Methylated spirit will dissolve shellac.

Before beginning any repair it is of primary concern that

all the broken edges must be absolutely clean. This may entail further soaking in hot water, if a water-soluble glue has been used, or dabbing with swabs of cotton wool moistened with methylated spirit, or acetone for other types of glue. If there are any obstinate pieces they can be carefully shifted with a scalpel or a finely pointed knife. Old dental probes, if you can beg them from your dentist, are excellent. When you think that all the old adhesives have been removed, use a magnifying glass to make certain.

The obvious principle behind china repair is to have the pieces fitting as closely as possible. Therefore, before using any adhesive, try putting the fragments together dry in order to make sure that the fit is snug.

The new adhesive which is used should be kept to as small an amount as possible. It is a mistake to imagine that because a large amount of glue has been used, the joint will be stronger. If you are using a water-clear acetate glue, a little should be squeezed out on to a piece of glass, then a finger should be dipped into the glue and wiped along the broken edges of the first piece you are going to replace. A

Plastic adhesive tape holds the pieces in position

While the glue is setting, some pieces need support

finger is really the best way to spread the glue, as it will tend to force the glue into all the crevices. But do watch out, as some of the edges of a break can be sharp. If you do not want to use your finger, the glue can be spread with a soft steel palette knife. If you are using epoxy glues, it may be better to use a knife in any case so as to avoid the possibility of skin irritation.

Now try to bring the glued edges firmly together at the exact place. Pieces should be pressed together with a fair amount of force to try to achieve the essential hair-line. If you are mending a plate, for example, that has been broken into a fair number of pieces, do not allow any extra thickness on the joins, because if you do, you will find that when you are putting in the final piece it just will not fit.

Quickly wipe off any excess glue that has oozed out from the joins. Although many of the glues today are quick-setting, to attempt to hold the pieces in place even for a few minutes is unwise, as any hand will tremble under this strain. The easiest solution is to bind the fragments firmly in place with strips of inch-wide sticky plastic tape. Do not be sparing with this. Take the tape across in several directions to equalize the strain. If you are repairing a cup or bowl, or any other object of an awkward shape, it will need some support to assist not only in holding the piece during repair but for the setting period. This may be in the form of a small wooden box or stiff cardboard lid filled with dry sand or pieces of moist clay, or plastic modelling material is excellent. As far as possible, place the object so that gravity will tend to pull the pieces together rather than apart.

In the past, sometimes owing to the lack of strength of the earlier glues, big breaks were often reinforced with ugly wire rivets or staples. The practice was that the china had holes drilled in it each side of the crack and these wire fixings were glued in. The strength of present-day glues precludes the use of these rivets, and from an aesthetic point of view, it is better they should be removed if possible and the mend re-done. Generally, a good soaking in hot water will make it possible to gently lift them out, or if a shellac glue has been used, a swab soaked in methylated spirit and left on for a

A 'shell break'

The chipped part filled with proprietary china paste

few minutes should do the trick. If a synthetic glue has been used, acetone on the cotton wool should bring it away.

When the mend has hardened thoroughly, the binding tape can be pulled away. If there are any small ridges of excess glue standing up on the cracks, these can be very gently scraped away with a small scalpel. Do not attempt to wipe the excess with a solvent, as you may weaken the mend.

One of the most annoying breaks for a plate, cup or bowl is what is called a shell break, where a small flake is knocked off. This can happen all too easily with washing up, when handling, or in packing several objects together. Unfortunately, usually these small pieces are lost and the only course is to rebuild the damaged area. Before making a start, the chipped part should be thoroughly cleansed.

A filler should now be prepared. A hardware store may have a proprietary china paste. This generally comes in two tins, and equal quantities from each are kneaded together.

But it is easy to make up your own paste. The basic powder can be kaolin, marble flour, slate powder or titanium dioxide. The paste can be made by mixing one of these with an epoxy glue to a stiff consistency that will model without losing its shape. Press the paste into the break, but do not make it level with the rest of the surface at this stage. It is essential that the repair should be left standing slightly 'proud'; this will allow for shrinkage. Owing to the hard and fast setting nature of the epoxy paste, endeavour, as far as possible, not to let any of it spread outside the break area; if this happens and it sets hard, the removal can easily damage decorated pieces.

After a drying interval of at least twenty-four hours the levelling down of the mend can be carried out. Shave away excess with a scalpel and then smooth down with wet-and-dry paper. Again care must be taken that surrounding decorative work is not touched.

Shaving away excess filler with a scalpel

Painting in the pattern calls for skill and a steady hand

When you come to the retouching it is best to put on the overall ground colour first. With many pieces this will be white. This may sound simple but it can be the hardest tint to match; very seldom will an absolutely dead white be encountered. Artists' oil colours can be used, but it is better to use high-quality and finely ground dry-powder colours. These can be mixed with a few drops of clear synthetic picture varnish on a piece of glass. The consistency should be fairly liquid, compatible with covering power. If the paint is too stiff, you will get ridges of impasto which will be difficult to level.

The retouched repair should be left for at least a week to harden out and the final touch can be a coat of synthetic picture varnish or a proprietary polyurethane varnish.

## Glass

Glass, although it is seemingly very hard, is liable to deteriorate with excessive damp; this applies, in particular, to that produced prior to the seventeenth century. It should always be kept in the driest place available. Washing should be carried out in warm water with a little gentle detergent, working on one piece at a time. Rinsing can be in cold water, although if the glass is fragile and valuable it is better to do this in lukewarm water. Lastly, it should be carefully dried using either a piece of chamois or a soft linen cloth. Woolly or cotton cloths are no good, as specks of fluff will be left. Decanters, bottles or close-necked jugs can be conveniently dried-out, using a hair-dryer.

Minute scratches on the surface can be treated with jewellers' rouge powder, either mixed with a few drops of olive oil or methylated spirit. The rubbing on should be gentle and progress watched. Afterwards the area can be washed and then polished with a soft chamois.

## Decanters

Decanters, or other containers with stoppers, should not be put away with the stoppers in place. The mouths can be covered with a tissue. If a stopper does become jammed, do not attempt to force it out by severe twisting. A little

Using a hair-dryer to dry the inside of a decanter

Decanters often become stained with wine

methylated spirit, with either glycerine or olive oil, can be poured round the place where the stopper enters the decanter and left overnight. The next morning the stopper should come free, but if not, some very gentle tapping will assist.

Decanters are very prone to staining if wine dregs are left in them overlong. One way to treat this is to fill the vessel with warm water, to which a teaspoonful of vinegar has been added. Leave the fluid in the vessel for about twelve hours, afterwards drain and wash. If the stain continues to be obstinate, it can be treated with a 5 per cent solution of nitric or sulphuric acid. Wear rubber gloves and pour sufficient of the solution into the vessel to cover the stain. Then swirl the liquid round for two or three minutes and pour away. Lastly, rinse several times to be sure that all the acid has been removed. If a cloudiness still remains, it will probably mean that the surface has become damaged by damp and is deteriorating, which is a condition that unfortunately cannot be rectified.

## Repairing glass

A broken glass object is among the most difficult things to mend. Generally the thickness of the piece is much less than with china and therefore there is a smaller surface for the glue to hold on.

Epoxy glues as well as some water-clear acetates can be purchased in small tubes. The procedure is similar to china. First wash and degrease the fragments. When applying the glue, if with a finger, take care for sharp edges. The repair once done should be firmly bound with sticky plastic tape and left for at least twenty-four hours to harden. Excess adhesive should be removed with a scalpel.

One common break is to a wine glass stem and it is best here to use an epoxy glue as it has greater strength. Before starting this kind of repair it is a must that adequate cradling is provided. This can be done by using one of the modelling pastes obtainable from an art-shop. Put down on the table two lumps of the material at the right distance apart to hold

Removing stains with weak hydrochloric acid

A broken wine glass stem repaired with epoxy glue, bound with tape and cradled on modelling paste

the top of the glass and the base. Take time to make sure that the pieces will be held securely and that they are absolutely lined up. Next gently lift one part of the glass to allow room for the glue to be brushed into the break. Bring the two sections together and gently press towards each other. Wipe off excess glue and bind tightly with sticky plastic tape. Leave the repair to thoroughly harden out for three or four days. It is unwise to try to hasten events by applying heat, as with some glass this could precipitate a further break. After the required period remove the tape and gently clean off any other excess glue with a scalpel.

Stained glass can become fogged with interior atmospheres and outside, if in a damp situation, can be obscured with moulds. The simplest treatment here is to wipe over with a 5 per cent solution of ammonia, rinsing off with clean water and then drying. Avoid wiping the lead cames and on no account should even weak acids be used, as they will be destructive to the lead.

## Ivory

Ivory is a material that should generally be left alone. The yellowing and darkening is very often the natural result of time, or with Oriental pieces, it may have been intentionally applied.

Both ivory and bone can be damaged by moisture and heat, and any washing should be kept to a minimum. With a carving little more than dabbing with a piece of damp cotton wool wound round a wooden splint should be attempted with thorough drying afterwards. Small breaks can be repaired with a water-clear acetate glue, using minimal quantities. After-treatment can be carried out with a little almond oil.

As has been mentioned earlier, if it is desired to bleach ivory or bone with objects such as piano keys or knife and fork handles it can be done with 20 volume hydrogen peroxide mixed with some whiting to form a paste. Using a palette knife or brush, this paste can then be spread over the object and left on in the first instance for about five minutes. Remove to observe progress and repeat, if necessary, and then thoroughly rinse with swabs of cotton wool and water. Finally dry completely. This bleaching should preferably be done on a dry day.

Refitting a handle

## Cutlery

Bone and ivory handles of knives and forks usually become unseated through carelessness with washing-up. The knives and forks should never be completely submerged in the washing-up water. The correct procedure is either to wash them one at a time, keeping the handle clear of the water, or to stand them blade or fork down in a jam jar of water with the handles free. Most of these implements have been stuck in originally with an animal or vegetable glue, which will very quickly soften on contact with water.

To repair, the old adhesive must first of all be cleared from the hole in the handle. This can be done with a knitting-needle with some cotton wool wrapped round it, or by the gentle use of a small meat-skewer. If the blade or fork fits tightly into the handle, it can be refitted with just the use of a water-clear acetate glue. But if it is loose, a cement can be made using the same glue mixed with kaolin, marble-dust or whiting. This can be spread round the shaft and then the handle pushed back over it, lastly wiping away any excess.

## Carpets and rugs

Carpets and rugs, depending on their type and quality, are liable to fading from strong, direct sunlight and if of value they should, where possible, be protected from this. They are also damaged by dirt, which if it works right into them can weaken the fibres. They should be cleaned regularly either with a brush or cautiously with a vacuum cleaner; whichever method is used, care should be taken that the tufts are not subjected to undue tugging. Depending again on value and condition, a proprietary carpet-cleaner should be safe, if the instructions are adhered to. One precaution is to test for colour fastness. This can be done by placing a piece of white blotting-paper underneath and on top and then dabbing with a piece of cotton wool, moistened with warm water and soap. This will give an indication as to whether the colours will run or not.

Stains on carpets and rugs, if of a greasy or an oily nature, can generally be taken out by a little dabbing with cotton wool moistened with white spirit. But here again it is advisable to make a test for colour fastness.

Working on a stained carpet

An antique silk shawl damaged by dry cleaning

## Textiles
### Cleaning fabrics

The cleansing of woven and printed textiles should be approached with caution, as at times quite unexpected damage can be caused. Commercial dry-cleaners will normally take the best care that they can, but some of the cleaning fluids they use can cause deterioration to the fabric and also react to certain dyes that have been used. If dealing with a delicate and valuable fabric, seek professional advice.

If treating at home, a fastness test, as with rugs and carpets, should always be given. For fabrics that are fixed, as with upholstery, the safest method is to gently dab with cotton wool moistened with white spirit. It should be remembered that this is inflammable and it is best to take the chair, or whatever is being treated, out of doors, as this will also allow for a quicker evaporation of the spirit. Upholstery can also be cleaned, using a commercial cleaning fluid specified for the purpose. The liquid can be brushed on or dabbed and then removed as directed and the area dried with towelling.

The washing of fabrics should always be carried out with a good quality soap or gentle detergent. It is unwise to fall back on legendary recipes from the past that include substances such as oxgall and horse-radish; the results from these are dubious and their after-effects can be still more in doubt.

The bath tub chosen should be as large as possible and the water soft. To start with, water alone can be tried. The fabric should be placed on a large sheet of plastic and lowered into the bath, the temperature of the water being no more than just lukewarm. The material can be left to soak for up to half an hour. During that time the water should be changed. Gentle kneading with the fingers is permissible. If, after this preliminary wash, the dirt is not loosened then the detergent can be added and further gentle squeezing given. When it appears that the fabric is as clean as one can get it, this should be followed by several rinsings, and after all traces of detergent have disappeared, the fabric – still on the plastic sheet – can be lifted from the bath.

Lowering a table mat on a plastic sheet into a warm bath

Manipulating the mat in the warm water

The fabric and plastic should now be laid flat on a table and excess moisture carefully dabbed off with dry towelling. A hair-dryer can also be used to accelerate the process. When it is still damp the fabric should be smoothed into its correct shape and then left to dry in a well ventilated warm room.

Textiles of any nature should always be stored in relative humidity, as near as possible to 65 per cent. If the atmosphere is too dry, it can tend to make the fibres brittle. If it is too damp and there is a lack of ventilation, conditions will encourage the growth of moulds. Ventilation is important, and occasionally it will be found with cupboards in old houses that stagnant pockets of air exist; these can sometimes be corrected by the boring of small holes at the bottom and top of the cupboard doors.

## Moth-proofing

A further menace, particularly with animal fibre fabrics, is moth. It is not the actual moth that does the damage but the larva. As with woodworm, cleanliness, such as the removal of all dust from the cupboard, will discourage this pest, as it likes to lay its eggs in dirt-filled cracks. Dirty fabrics should never be stored as they are a great attraction to the female moth.

There are a great many commercial anti-moth and insect repellents on the market, and most are completely safe for fabrics. The instructions should, however, be read with care as some of the liquids, crystals and powders can be toxic. If putting away textiles for a lengthy period, a good plan is to seal them in plastic bags with the addition of some anti-moth chemicals. Textiles should always be rolled for storage, as tight folding for long periods can weaken the fibres on the folds.

When fabrics are taken out of storage they should always be taken outside to be shaken free of any remaining crystals, and then be left hanging in a well ventilated space until free of smell. This also applies to materials that have been to commercial dry-cleaners.

Moth-proofing preparations can also be purchased and are

Lifting the plastic sheet from the bath

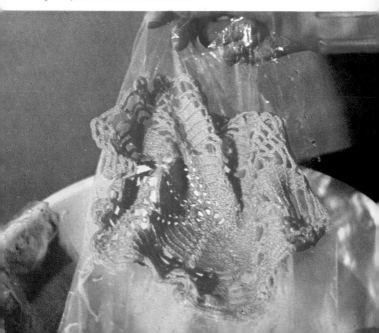

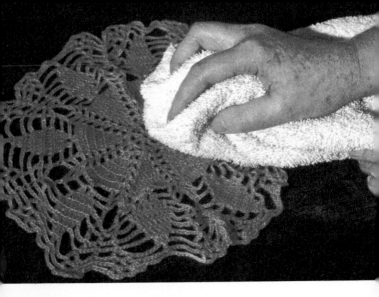

Moisture should be dabbed off with a towel

usually harmless. When using these on upholstered furniture, where there are polished arms or legs, one must take care, as the proofing liquids may contain a solvent which will attack the polish and quite quickly go through it, therefore all wooden areas should be masked before spraying.

## Tapestries

The cleaning of tapestries is very much the province of the specialist. Damage can very easily be caused. Nothing more than a brushing down with a soft brush should be undertaken in the home.

It is essential that a tapestry should be displayed correctly. All too often one comes across examples of tapestries that have been stretched all round on a wooden frame in the manner of a canvas for oil painting. This is injurious as it can cause the material to be distorted. A tapestry was originally intended to hang, supported only from the top. Further, it may have been tacked on with iron or steel tacks which can quickly rust. Examine the mounting and have it rectified as soon as possible. If the tapestry is weak, it is best that it should be supported on some strong nylon net, which will help to take and distribute the weight. The net itself can be fixed to a top stretcher and then the material fixed to it. In general this fixing should be done by careful sewing, rather than the use of any adhesives that could cause discolouration.

## Embroidery

Embroidery of any type should always be carefully inspected for soundness and also in a corner a fastness test can be applied. If this is positive, gentle washing, as with fabrics, can be carried out. It can also be treated with white spirit. If possible, a flat photographic developing dish should be used and the material gently pushed with the finger-tips. Liquids like benzene and carbon tetrachloride should never be used, as although they are good cleaners, both are highly dangerous to the operative.

If a silver thread is present in the embroidery, diluted solutions of ammonia can be tried to remove the tarnish,

Carefully smoothing the mat while still damp

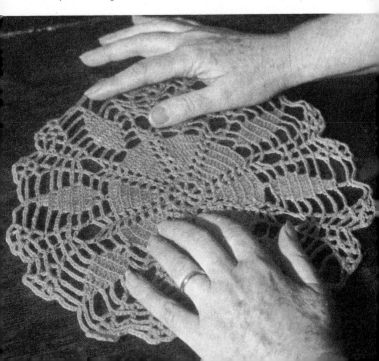

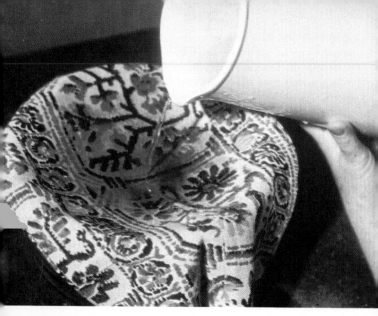

Removing a coffee stain with very hot water

being increased to produce the required result. Afterwards adequate rinsing must take place. This method should not be used where the material has been dyed. A second course is to apply a silver-dip liquid, putting it on with a small paint-brush. Here the dip should not be allowed to touch the rest of the piece and thorough rinsing must finish the process.

Some homes have had samplers passed down from previous generations. These are often on a coarse linen or wool thread base and should be tested, as described earlier, for the possibility of colours running. If safe, they can be cleansed with water and detergent in a flat dish. If the colours show signs of running, they can be dry-cleaned using white spirit. But if the sampler is in a delicate state with slight rotting, no dry-cleaning or washing should be attempted. The only course open is to dust the surface with warmed potato flour which should then be gently brushed off; the sequence can be repeated and will often shift much grime.

The best way to mount a sampler is to buy an artist's wooden canvas stretcher from your art dealer. On this wooden frame a piece of linen should be stretched that will tone in with the sampler. The stretching should be done by using copper tacks. Then the sampler can be smoothed on to this surface and sewn round the edges with fine silk or cotton that will, as nearly as possible, match the basic colour of the piece. The final framing can be with a suitable plain wooden moulding, glazing and an adequate backing.

## Removing stains

Costumes, curtains, upholstery attract a wide variety of stains during their life, and many can be very obstinate to remove, particularly if they have been left for some time.

What is important before making a start is to identify the stain. Coffee is one of the most common stains. If you catch it at once, the mark should come away with an application of warm water and borax; finish by washing with mild detergent and plenty of rinsing. If there is a grease mark left from milk or cream, this should be dabbed with white spirit. Old coffee

Treating iron mould on a table cloth

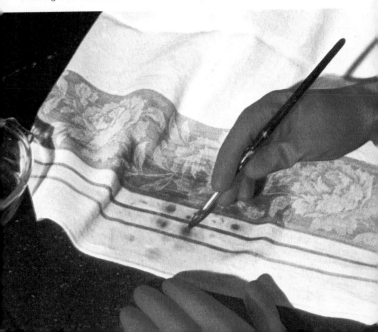

Candle-wax may be removed with blotting-paper and a warm iron

stains should first be damped with water and then have glycerine rubbed into them which should be left on for about an hour before being rinsed. A fabric that is firm, which has just had tea spilt on it, should be stretched over a bowl and have very hot water poured on the stain. Lemon juice can often loosen an old tea stain.

Ink stains will normally dissolve with an application of table salt and lemon juice. A more drastic treatment is to dab the mark with oxalic acid and then thoroughly rinse. Ball-point pen marks should have an application of methylated spirit.

One of the worst offenders on any fabric is iron mould. If the material is fragile great care is needed. The causes of this stain are various but most of them are associated with damp. First moisten the stain and the area around with distilled water and then apply a 2 per cent solution of 'Chloramine T'. Work this into the mark with a soft paint-brush. Follow up with a 5 per cent solution of oxalic acid and almost at once rinse very thoroughly with several applications of distilled water. The reason for damping the area outside the stain is to prevent a ring-mark when the material has dried.

Chocolate or cocoa stains should respond to gentle washing with warm water and detergent, to which a little ammonia has been added. Fruit stains, if caught at once, will generally come away with plenty of hot water. If this fails, 5 per cent oxalic acid can be tried and then well rinsed away. Fabrics stained with milk should be well washed first in water as hot as can be used with safety, with a detergent, and then dabbed with white spirit.

If candle-wax is dripped on to a fabric the excess should first be scraped away with a blunt edge, then white blotting-paper placed underneath and on top of the mark. Using a thermostatically controlled iron, set at a safe heat for the type of fabric being treated, apply the iron for a few seconds. If all the wax has not been lifted, use two more sheets of

Hot potato flour is used on delicate lace

The potato flour is brushed off after a few minutes

clean blotting-paper and repeat the process. If small traces are still left, these can be dabbed with cotton wool and white spirit. Grease and oil marks may be given the same treatment. For small grease marks that have recently fallen on to a material it can be found that a dusting with fuller's earth will be sufficient.

Lace is very easy to damage when cleaning. If washed, shrinkage can occur; threads can be pulled by thoughtless handling. The safest course is to resort to a dry-powder cleaning. The piece of lace should be carefully spread out on clean paper. Then in a saucepan gently heat some potato flour to a temperature that the hand can just bear. Spoon out the potato flour so that it will form a layer about half an inch deep over the lace and tamp it down. Leave until it is cool and then remove with a soft brush. A second application can be made.

This same treatment can be given to most delicate embroideries although it is not advised for stump-work, as it can be very difficult to brush out the flour.

## Sculpture

Today stone statues outside, even in the cleaner atmospheres, all too soon wrap themselves in an obscuring veil of grime. Those made from limestone or granite can be quite freely treated with water. Hoses can be left playing on them for twenty-four hours or more, and then they can be scrubbed with a wire-brush dipped in a weak solution of ammonia.

Limestone and marble that have become stained with bad patches of green mildew can be treated by using a poultice method. Some cheap white paper should be torn up and then put into a metal bucket with water; this should be well heated and then given a thorough beating to produce a mash-like consistency. When cool it should be spread over the stained area to a thickness of about half an inch. As it dries, evaporation will tend to draw out the blemishes. The same principle can be followed using a material called 'sepiolite' or kaolin to form the paste. If the stain has a grease or wax base, the poultice can still be used. This time, after it has been prepared, it should be allowed to dry out and then remixed with white spirit before applying.

A special poultice will draw stains out of limestone or marble

Old varnish makes paintings dark and dull

## Oil paintings

The large majority of oil paintings have been carried out on either canvas or wooden panels. The general rule is that these are always first primed with a coat of white lead or similar substance; with wooden panels this grounding generally consists of *gesso*, which is a mixture of a glue and plaster. Further the canvas is given a brushing over with size to render it non-absorbent to oil. The artist may build up his pictures with several layers of paint, starting with weak thin applications and finishing with heavy paint with rich textural ridges known as *impasto*. Finally after a lengthy drying period the picture will be varnished. All of which points to the fact that a painting can be a complicated sandwich of different materials and so should be placed in a room with regard to conditions of light and particularly heat. An oil painting should never be hung over a heat source, as this is bound to cause a movement of the support and layers as the temperature rises and falls. Moreover, dust and grime, carried up by the draughts from the heater, will be sprayed over the picture.

In the past the varnishes used were all made from natural resins such as copal, damar, and mastic. All of these, to a degree, will crack and darken with time. The darkening is generally a gradually intensifying deep yellow tone, that eventually will completely change the whole aspect of a painting. Blues become dirty dark greens, whites are obscured and flesh tints altered considerably. The cracking of the varnish also attracts surface dirt which sticks into the interstices. In some cases the varnish layers are considerably thicker than the paint underneath, as it has been the custom just to slap on another coat of varnish when a picture became obscured. This, for a short time, will tend to revivify the old varnish so that details can be seen, but it very soon darkens again.

Expert cleaning can have a dramatic effect

A proprietary cleaner will remove surface dirt

Many of the natural resin varnishes become extremely hard and call for strong solvents to remove them. As these same solvents will quite clearly attack the oils holding the paint, this is a treatment that should never be attempted unless by a professional restorer. A few seconds, literally, of ignorant application and a priceless painting can be ruined!

If an oil painting is of no great value, a form of surface cleaning can be attempted in the home. The surface of the varnish will in time accumulate a fairly heavy layer of airborne dirt and grease from the atmosphere. The painting should be put on an easel, if available, if not, propped upright securely. A piece of cotton wool moistened with white spirit can be gently applied to a small area of the picture. It is best to make a start at the edge of the canvas which comes underneath the rabbet of the frame.

It is important that no real pressure should be put on to the swab of cotton wool, because if the painting is on canvas this could cause cracking and if it is scrubbed violently, it could cause scratching. You should work over an area of about two square inches at a time, inspecting the cotton wool frequently to see if any paint is being lifted, and if it is, stop at once. If the picture is sound, there should be no untoward effects, and you will find that quite considerable quantities of dirt will come away in the form of a greyish mess on the cotton wool. Continue the treatment, as evenly as possible, over the whole of the picture area.

There are a number of proprietary picture cleaners that can be purchased from an art shop. Normally these are safe if the instructions with them are followed implicitly. It should be emphasized that these are, in principal, surface cleaners and will not remove varnish. They will, however, tend to get off much more of the surface grime than the white spirit treatment.

It is important that you keep these cleaners well shaken whilst you are working. They should be applied with cotton wool and worked from the edge of a painting, as with the

The picture should be cleaned in small sections

When clean and dry, the painting can be revarnished

white spirit. You should constantly inspect the swabs and as soon as they become dirty, throw them away and use fresh ones. It is false economy to go on using an over-dirty swab, as you will not be able to see if paint is coming away. As each area of the picture is cleaned, it should be thoroughly rinsed by using more cotton wool dipped in white spirit.

When the painting has dried out, it can be revarnished. Although natural resin varnishes can still be bought, it is better to choose one of the water-clear synthetic resin varnishes, as they are less likely to darken or yellow; they are also less likely 'to bloom'; and, as many of them have a plasticizer incorporated in them, they should not crack.

Varnishing should be carried out on a dry day and in as dust-free an atmosphere as possible. The painting can be treated either placed on an easel or lying flat on a table. It is important that there is an adequate light source, so that the application of the varnish can be watched, to make sure that no small areas are missed.

Varnishes can be bought in aerosol tins, but spraying does need experience if an even layer is to be attained. For the inexperienced it is probably better in any case to use a special varnish brush. This should be flat and about two inches wide with good quality white hog bristle. Before buying, establish that the bristles are firmly in place.

Pour out a little of the varnish into a clean saucer and start working from one edge of the picture. Avoid putting on too much varnish and try to keep the application even. This can best be done by using criss-cross strokes. Keep the application moving smartly, particularly with a large canvas, as it will be found that some of the synthetic varnishes start drying quite quickly. Hardening time can vary between one hour and twelve hours. During this period it is essential that the picture should be kept away from dust and not moved.

The varnishes that can be bought have varying finishes, ranging from very high gloss down to mat surfaces. There are also available jars of picture wax which may be constituted from white beeswax or synthetic waxes. These soft pastes are generally best applied with pieces of fluff-free cotton or linen rags and depending on the instructions are normally left on for a period of time, then the excess is wiped off and the surface gently polished.

Folds in the canvas will disfigure a painting

Tapping the wedges of a stretcher to remove folds in the canvas

Sometimes disfiguring folds appear in paintings on canvas. These are caused either by the canvas coming away from the stretcher or by a movement of the stretcher itself. In the past varying types of wooden stretchers have been used. The earliest examples were often plain wooden frames with some form of simple corner jointing and with no provision for adjustment. From the nineteenth century onwards it became general practice to use wooden stretchers with some form of sliding joint in the corners, into which wedges could be driven.

If the canvas which has developed folds is stretched on this type of frame, it can normally be quite easily rectified. First it should be inspected to see that it is quite firm and is adequately tacked at the edges. It should then be stood on edge on a firm bench or table and the wedges gently tapped using a small hammer. Repeat the process, turning the picture round, and observe progress. Do not aim to achieve a drumlike tightness however, as this could damage the paint layers.

Very often iron or steel tacks have been used to fix the canvas to the stretcher and in damp atmospheres these quite quickly rust and cause rotting. If the canvas is otherwise sound, the old tacks should be carefully levered out, one at a time, and replaced with copper tacks. A stapler can also be used, but only with copper staples.

If the painting is of value and the canvas is in a bad state, it should be treated by an expert, who will re-line. This means that he will fix the old canvas on to a new canvas. This is normally done using an adhesive of beeswax and damar resin, which is melted either with an iron or on a hot vacuum table. Not only does this provide a fresh strong support for the picture, but also the melted wax adhesive will impregnate the whole depth of the painting, consolidating all the layers of priming and paint.

If a picture is torn, help should be sought as soon as possible. It is vitally important that the tear should not be neglected, as the edges of the canvas will start to curl and quite considerable paint losses will occur. Do not apply any adhesive tape to the surface of the painting. At most, just secure the tear at the back of the canvas with a piece of sticky plastic tape.

Paintings on wooden panels are particularly suspect to changes in humidity and temperature. Those painted in the sixteenth century, even if of a large size, were often on quite thin panels, ranging between quarter and half an inch in thickness. They will very quickly, even after centuries, react to atmosphere changes and start to warp.

Replacing old iron tacks with new copper ones

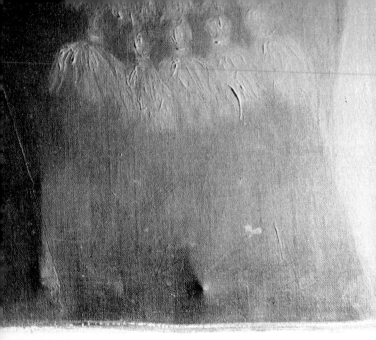
Bumps and dents sometimes appear in a canvas

When a framed canvas is hanging on the wall it is possible that considerable quantities of dirt can accumulate in between the back of the canvas and the wooden stretcher. Holly berries from Christmas decorations can become lodged, also bits of plaster from an old ceiling, and these can quite soon cause unsightly bumps to appear on the surface of the painting. Loose wedges have been known to drop out and get stuck in the same manner, and in one case, with a very large canvas, a long oblong bump turned out to be, for some obscure reason, the butler's fountain-pen.

If these conditions are noticed, a table should be prepared with a covering of clean soft cloth. The picture should be taken down and removed from the frame and laid face down on the table. If possible procure a long-bladed crank-handled painting knife and very gently slide this in between the canvas and the stretcher, at the same time slightly lifting the edge of the picture. Now carefully ease the obstructions free and scrape them clear.

Unglazed oil paintings should not, in general, be subjected to dusting with cloths, as this may scratch the sometimes delicate surface, or if there is impasto it can be broken loose or pick up threads from the cloth. At most, dusting should not consist of more than the gentle use of a feather duster.

Oil paintings are still, unfortunately, subjected to some pretty rough handling. There are many homespun recipes which include the use of cut potatoes and onions and even washing with soap and water. One of the most extreme cases I know of was when quite a fine eighteenth-century portrait was brought along for treatment with the face nearly missing. There were only vestiges of the features left and in places the canvas had been almost wiped clean. The owner innocently explained that he had had a go himself using a bath-scouring powder! The answer with all these makeshift remedies is 'don't'. Water in any form can penetrate the layers. It can cause varnish to disintegrate. It can cause the size to swell, and very soon bring about blistering where the paint layers become loose and will flake away.

A canvas can often be slightly dented in moving or by a careless knock when it is on the wall or when it is in storage. If this is severe enough to cause cracking of the paint layers, it should be treated professionally. If, however, the dent is quite small, it may be possible to remedy it oneself. Once again the picture should be taken off the wall and out of the

A small object being removed from between stretcher and canvas

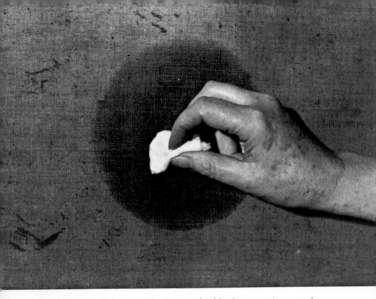

A small dent being gently removed with damp cotton wool

frame and then the defect can be carefully wiped on the back of the canvas with a small swab of cotton wool moistened with water. The damping should be kept to a minimum amount and the application be little more than a caress carried out with a circular motion working from the centre of the dent to a distance of about 3 or 4 inches away from it. Do not apply even gentle heat to assist the drying. Leave this to be done naturally.

In some homes, particularly on hot summer evenings, small birds can fly through the open windows. They will often perch on the tops of frames and can soil the surface of unglazed paintings with their droppings, which are not only unsightly but can, if left, cause damage to the paint, bleaching some colours. If the droppings are detected in good time, it is best to remove them with a piece of cotton wool, slightly moistened with white spirit. If they have been left on for a considerable time, they should be given professional treatment.

Fly spots are also a nuisance, as apart from being ugly they too can affect the paint. If they are fresh they should respond to cotton wool and white spirit, but if they are hardened, they will probably have to be carefully and professionally removed with a small scalpel.

## Framing

It is sad to see that it is almost universal practice to fix oil paintings, whether on canvas or on wooden panels, into frames by the use of nails. Sometimes these are actually driven right through the stretcher and into the frame. The concussion from the use of a hammer can obviously affect a delicate painting. It can also damage a gesso-decorated frame.

The ideal way of fixing a picture in a frame should be to allow for some movement. The best plan is to buy some brass strip about three-quarters of an inch wide, and to cut it into 2 inch lengths and then to drill a hole in one end. You should screw this to the frame, having bent the strip so that it will fit snugly across the frame and on to the picture stretcher. If brass strip cannot be found, what are called 'shelf ears' are a very good substitute. They generally have two holes which can be fixed on to the frame. The amount of fastenings needed will depend on the size of the picture. With one measuring about 25 × 30 inches, one on each side should normally be sufficient.

Shelf ears' will hold a painting in its frame

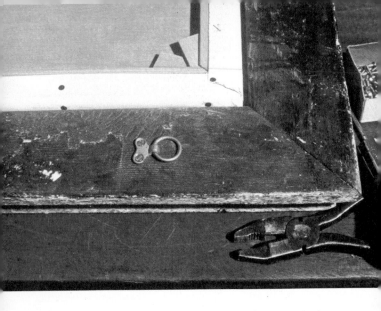

A brass plate and ring is best for attaching the chain to the frame

Hanging wires or chains should always be given a regular inspection, as in damp atmospheres they can deteriorate. Generally speaking, especially with larger pictures, it is better to use a good quality picture chain, because not only is this aesthetically more pleasing, but it is also simpler to hang a picture level just by equalizing the number of links.

The chain can be attached to the frame by steel screw-eyes with split-rings, or better still, by a small brass plate and ring. The fixtures should be placed about one-third of the way down the frame from the top. This will allow the picture to hang with a slight forward cant. This not only makes the picture easier to view, particularly if it has a high-gloss varnish, but also helps to prevent dust from accumulating on the paint surface.

String and cord are not really suitable for hanging pictures, as they can stretch and also quite quickly rot if they have been tied over steel screw-eyes which are rusting.

One point to watch when fixing picture lights is that there is not too much cable that can become bundled up and pressed into the back of the canvas. The lights can be fixed either at the top of the frame or the bottom. If it is at the bottom, the fitting should stand out far enough from the frame so that undue heat from the lamp cannot play on the painting. Another effective manner of lighting a particular picture, or several in a group, can be to have a fixture on the ceiling and to use one of the large bulbs with a built-in reflector.

It is always worth the expense of protecting the back of a valuable canvas when in a frame. This can be done with a piece of hardboard cut about an inch wider, all the way round, than the picture. It should have a series of small ventilation holes drilled at the top and at the bottom and then it can be screwed into place. On this backing can be fixed any labels giving details of the artist and the picture.

If the stretcher has become worm-eaten, it should never be given a treatment with woodworm liquid, as this may seep through and attack the painting. It is best to have the stretcher replaced. Likewise, worm-eaten frames should always be removed from pictures before treatment.

A protective hardboard back should have ventilation holes at top and bottom

Cork on the bottom corners will protect the wall

If the pictures are hanging on an expensive wallpaper or painted walls, they can quite easily injure the surface. This can be prevented by placing a piece of cork on the two bottom corners of the frame. It is not necessary to use more than just a touch of glue. This course incidentally also assists the ventilation round the painting.

Today the fashion for heavily gilt frames is going out. With some of the older paintings, there is a return to plain mouldings in dark, natural wood. For a modern picture, the finishes which suit them best often incorporate light warm greys, with here and there perhaps a little gold showing through.

If you have an antique gilt frame which is carved or built up with cast gesso, it can be very fragile. Small scratches, or tiny chips, can generally be covered up with a touch of gilding. But if a fragment of the gesso has broken off, it should be refixed with a water-clear acetate glue and whilst hardening held in place with sticky plastic tape. Should the gesso piece be missing, it will have to be built up. Gesso powder that only needs the addition of water can be bought, but if you want to make your own, you can do it with whiting mixed with either diluted size, Scotch glue or rabbit's-skin glue. This should be done hot in a double boiler and the consistency varied according to the task.

When the part missing is in a corner of the frame and of a considerable size, a few panel pins should be driven half-way into the wood to act as a support. The stiff gesso can be modelled roughly into shape and then, after it has hardened for about an hour, the modelling can be continued with a small palette knife or scalpel.

Small cracks can be filled in by pushing the gesso into them with a finger-tip and then wiping off any excess. Once the gesso has thoroughly hardened, which will take about twenty-four hours, it can be further scraped into shape with a scalpel and then smoothed down with a piece of fine sand-paper. Whilst doing this, try to avoid injuring the surrounding areas.

Before going further, the gesso should be given a coat of an isolator, as it is very porous. The isolator can be made by dissolving shellac to saturation point in methylated spirit, or

Repairing a damaged frame by modelling gesso with a scalpel

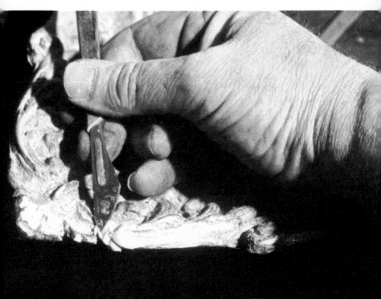

White gesso should be given a coat of isolator followed by burnt umber

a coat of size will suffice. Before applying any gilding, paint over the new gesso in a fairly rich tone of burnt umber, using artists' oil-colour diluted with white spirit. This is to provide a ground.

The most expensive gold frames are gilt with gold leaf. It is a skilled process to apply, as the leaf is very thin and difficult to manoeuvre. For some repairs you will have to fall back on gold paint which you can buy at the store. This may be either in liquid or paste form and can normally be bought in a number of gold shades, so that you should be able to match the exact tint of your frame.

The paste golds can be rubbed on with a finger-tip or a piece of cotton wool or rag. The liquid preparations need to be very well shaken and they can then be applied best with a small soft-haired brush, which will need to be cleaned out· well afterwards with acetone or white spirit. If the fresh gilding stands out like a 'sore thumb' when it is dry, it can be brushed over with raw umber, or burnt umber, diluted with white spirit. Finally, when this is firm the area can be lightly polished with a little wax.

Simple moulded frames are cheaper if you make them yourself. You will need some form of carpenter's bench with a mitre clamp to guide the saw when making the cuts, and also when fixing the corners. Small frames can generally quite adequately be fixed using an epoxy glue. Larger ones should be given the added strength of a screw. Your local timber merchant will generally carry a fair selection of mouldings. A hard wood, such as oak, need have little more treatment than perhaps a light staining with oil, and when this is dry can be given a wax polish. Softer woods, such as pine, are best given a coat of fairly liquid gesso. This can be brushed on smooth, lightly stippled with a brush, or textural effects can be made with a comb. When the gesso has hardened, it should be isolated. The final treatment can consist of broken effects achieved with several different tones of distemper. Or it can be gilt first and then have the distemper put on the top and gently wiped with a piece of cotton wool damped with water to let a little of the gold show through, and last of all given a slight polish with wax.

Applying gold paint to the repaired corner

Inserting a fillet

Sometimes the appearance of certain pictures and frames can be considerably improved by the insertion of a fillet. This should consist of a thin flat slip of wood or stout card cut with mitred corners to fit in between the frame and painting. The width can vary with the effect required. Normally you should aim to have about half an inch showing all the way round.

A fillet can be of hard or soft wood. The former can look well lightly polished or limed. Soft woods are better given a coat of emulsion flat paint. The colour can vary from near-white to fairly deep warm greys, ecru and porridge. Another device is to cover the fillet with rough or smooth linen, coarse canvas or velvet. The fabric can be stuck down with animal glue or acetate.

There is another use for a fillet. At times a frame may be picked up which is just too large for a painting that you have.

The insertion of a slightly wider fillet than usual can rectify the discrepancy. The picture can be held firm in the frame with small blocks of wood gummed to the back of the rabbet or with pieces of cork.

## Prints

Whether you decide to clean a print should certainly be influenced by the value. If it is a Dürer or a Rembrandt, the answer must be to leave it to the expert. Such examples are now often exceedingly valuable and the risk is not worth taking.

If you do think that some black and white prints of little value can be treated, provide yourself with a good stock of white blotting paper, because this will be needed with all the methods which can be used.

If by chance candle wax has got on a print, it should first be scraped off, as far as possible, with a blunt edge, with the print lying on a sheet of glass. The print can then be placed between two sheets of blotting-paper and a reasonably hot iron applied. This technique can also be used for grease or oil spots. Tiny traces of residue should surrender to white spirit. However, with very stubborn grease, pyridine can be spotted on with a soft brush.

If the print is generally grimy, it may be washed. Before taking this step, you should gently test the ink to be certain that it is not water-soluble. The print can then be put on a sheet of glass and lowered into a large photographic develop-

Removing grease from a print between two sheets of blotting-paper

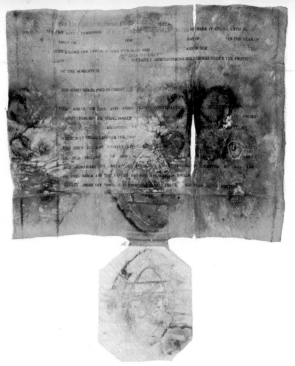

An extreme case of foxing on an old document

ing dish. You should then pour into the tray to the depth of about half an inch distilled water to which has been added a few drops of a gentle detergent. At first this can be swilled across the print and then the print should be gently stroked with a large soft water-colour mop-brush. Never approach a scrubbing action. Pour off the detergent and water and give three or four rinsings. Then lift the print from the dish, still on the glass, and carefully transfer it to a clean sheet of blotting-paper. When laid flat on a drawing-board it can have a second sheet of blotting-paper laid on the top which is gently tamped to start the drying. Use several sheets of blotting-paper until the print is almost bone-dry. It can then be finished by the pressure of a warm iron through yet more blotting-paper.

Dry-cleaning can be tried with slightly dirty prints. The surface can be caressed with a piece of gum eraser or with a lump of kneaded new bread. The back, as well as the front, should be treated.

One of the most unsightly and annoying troubles with prints, and for that matter any works on paper, is 'foxing'. This makes itself known by the appearance of small orange-brown spots that can sometimes grow wide enough to almost obscure much of the fine work. They are more likely to come on old papers in which the size has broken down and forms a useful breeding ground for the fungus spores that are at the back of the pest.

If the 'foxing' is confined to a few isolated spots an attempt can be made to bleach them out using equal parts of hydrogen peroxide and methylated spirit. This should be applied with a small soft brush. Watch carefully and as the stain starts to shift, blot and repeat until it has gone. Lastly, give several rinses with distilled water, again using the brush. If the specimen has bad overall 'foxing' it will have to be treated in a dish. Place on a sheet of glass and lower into the

Gross microbiological attack on book illustration

In a mount the proportions of the margins are vital

dish which should have about half an inch of a solution of Chloramine T in distilled water. The strength should not be more than about 3 per cent. The progress should be watched, and when sufficiently advanced the bleach is poured away and several rinsings given in clean, distilled water. The print should then be lifted out on the glass and placed between sheets of white blotting-paper for drying.

If a print has been varnished, it is sometimes safe to remove this with a mixture of white spirit and methylated spirit. Thorough tests for the fastness of the ink should be made first. After treatment it should be rinsed with white spirit to remove all traces of the stronger solvent.

Unfortunately a large number of prints have been mounted by sticking the whole of the back on to often cheap cardboard. If this has been done with animal glue it can encourage foxing. If the ink is fast to water, a gentle soaking in warm water should make it possible to free the print from the mount.

Before remounting any prints that have been treated, a wise step is to wipe over the backs with a solution of thymol. This will stop further attacks of foxing.

Water-colours, pastels and drawings can so easily be damaged that home treatment should not be attempted.

## Mounting

Any print or drawing really deserves a mount. Even if it is only kept in a folio, this is still important, as it will help to protect the picture. Mounting cards vary considerably in thickness, colour and quality. Where possible, the best quality ones should be chosen. The proportion of mount to print is important. Broadly speaking, the width of the mount at the top and the two sides should be the same, and the width at the bottom about half an inch more. When measuring for the window of the mount, allow for enough space to show the plate mark and of course any numbering at the bottom, and if present, the artist's signature.

The cutting of the mount should be done with a sharp modelling knife held at an angle of about 45 degrees to achieve the bevel. The fixing of the print into the mount should be done using four strips of thin white paper, these are called guards, which are lightly pasted to the edge of the print and on to the mount. If the print is slightly buckled, it can be gently moistened with a small sponge before fixing to the mount. As it dries, it will tighten.

The first stage in attaching a print to its mount

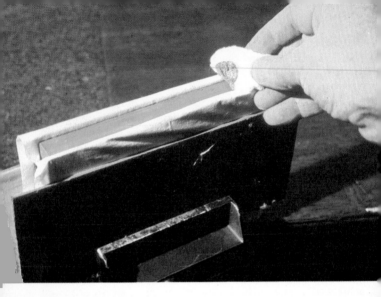

To clean the edges of the pages, a book must be tightly clamped

## Books

Leather bound books can be treated with the leather dressing in the Recipes section of this book, and, if desired, after three or four days can be given an extra polish with beeswax.

General grime on the pages will often come away when it is gently rubbed with a finger-tip dipped into potato flour. A piece of artist's gum erazer can be used and stale bread-crumbs can be tried. Grease spots can be worked over with a small brush dipped in ether or white spirit. Before doing this, remember to put a piece of grease-proof paper or other protectant under the page.

Small tears can be mended using a cornflour paste to which has been added a drop of formaldehyde or thymol. With a small brush touch along the edges of the tear, bringing the two edges together; then place a piece of lens tissue on each side and put a piece of wax paper on each side of the page. Now close the book and leave to set. When the paste has hardened, the excess tissue can be removed and the area gently rubbed with potato flour to render the mend as transparent as possible.

To clean page edges, the book should first be put into some form of clamp that will ensure all the pages are held tightly together. If the edges have been gilt, they can first be dusted off with a piece of cotton wool and then wiped with another piece dipped in ether. If the gilding has become damaged, it may be possible to brighten it up by using one of the gold pastes already mentioned. Where the page-edges have not been gilt or coloured, they can be first dusted and then gently rubbed with a piece of very fine sand-paper.

## Household hints

The effect of heat was mentioned earlier, and it is a subject which needs a certain amount of planning to combine comfort with safety for possessions. It is all too easy, when a cold spell comes, to use extra appliances and overlook the piece of furniture they are near to, or the condition they are creating. Electric fan-heaters can expel a rather hot blast of dry air, which if it is allowed to play on to a piece of veneered furniture can accelerate lifting and cracking. This type of heater should only be used where there is plenty of space to dissipate the hot, dry air. Oil stoves and gas fires can both have a considerable drying effect on the atmosphere.

If you are moving house, it is a wise plan to sketch out in

Furniture should not be near a stove

These books will soon be damaged by the dry heat

advance the lay-out of the rooms, showing fixed heating appliances, also probable positions of movable heaters and windows and doors which could cause lines of draught. The placing of the principal and most valuable pieces can then be worked out. When the transition is from a very damp atmosphere to a comparatively dry one, heating and air-conditioning should be brought in slowly, so that the pieces of furniture, in particular, will acclimatize themselves to the change in humidity. If this is not done, and there is much difference between the conditions of the old and the new house, a likelihood exists that not only veneers and inlays will be affected, but also carcass wood underneath, and solid wood furniture.

Excessive dryness from heating appliances, radiators and air-conditioning plants can be alleviated by some form of humidifier that allows for a gradual evaporation of moisture into the atmosphere. The simplest type is one which can be hung directly on to a radiator. This humidifier may be made of earthenware or more sophisticated kinds in this category are thin perforated metal boxes containing a large absorbent wick. With both these, the reservoir compartments are simply filled with water, at whatever interval is suggested in the instructions. There are also available on the market a number of electrically operated humidifiers. The simplest of these is a form of heater with a container of water over it which can replace up to a pint of moisture per hour in the atmosphere. The more expensive models include fans to assist the circulation, and the amount of moisture expelled can be controlled.

It is well worth the small extra expense of having in the main room of a house instruments which will accurately record the humidity and temperature. This may sound complicated, but if a watch can be kept on these factors, much damage will be avoided.

Practically every household has at least a few objects – china, furniture, glass, paintings, silver – which have intrinsic, aesthetic or just sentimental value. It will be seen by what has gone before that these can often be seriously damaged through careless handling, lack of knowledge or other reasons. In this bustling, pressured world it seems difficult to make a little time for extra jobs. But once a system has been started, it need not occupy too long a time in our already filled days.

A container of water on a radiator

Dust can be removed from crevices with a blower

After the control of heat and humidity should come an all-out battle for cleanliness. This is not just a fad or a health measure. Search out crevices and cracks that can hold dirt. The house will smell sweeter, insect pests will have less chance of finding ready-made nurseries. Inspect cupboards and places which are damp and have stagnant air.

Go through stored curtains, blankets, other textiles and furs, to be sure you are not harbouring an invasion of moths. If you do find signs of this, be sure to take the affected pieces outside before brushing them. By the same token, examine upholstery, lifting up the squabs from sofas or chairs, and pulling the covers out of the crevices.

At least once a year the library should be gone through. Insect pests will attack bindings and paper. One of the first things to do is to give the books a thorough dusting – particularly the tops. Open them out to see if there is any sign of infestation. At the first evidence of deterioration in leather bindings treat them with dressing.

Where you have candlesticks or other similar objects on highly polished surfaces, inspect the bottoms and if the base pads have rotted, replace them.

Light is one of the most essential things for the enjoyment of your home. But strong sun-light can play havoc with the patina of furniture, paintings – especially water-colours – and a large number of types of fabrics. In hot climates some form of shielding should be provided to break up the direct light beams. This may be either in the form of an external canvas canopy, or a kind of Venetian blind that has adjustable slats. It is possible to buy glass that will keep out a large amount of the sunlight's ultra-violet rays. It is not cheap, but to protect a valuable painting it is worth the expense. It is also possible to obtain a varnish that contains an ultra-violet ray inhibiting agent. This can be sprayed or brushed on to windows.

Textiles to be stored should be rolled up with moth-proof crystals

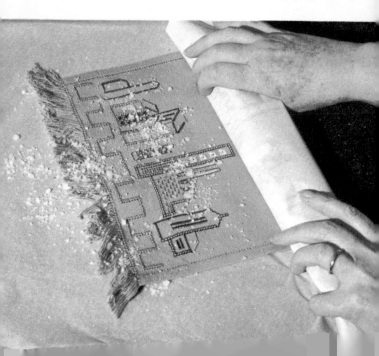

Strong sun-light can damage furniture and fabrics

It should not be forgotten that artificial light can also be harmful. Both tungsten and fluorescent lamps emit a noticeable amount of ultra-violet radiation. The latter gives out more, and if it is used to light an object of value, it should have some system for filtering.

Tungsten lights often generate a good deal of heat, depending upon the type of fitting. If this plays upon an object, it can cause gradual deterioration. One answer is to have fittings that have been specifically designed and tested for the purpose. Another is not to have too bright a bulb.

Nature's threats to works of art, as we have seen, include moisture, mould growths, insect attack and light. To these can be added careless handling, ignorance, and pollution. Although this last menace has grown in the twentieth century to an enormous dimension, sadly enough, its harm still seems not to be appreciated by many.

# Pollution

The incomplete combustion of fuels, the burning of wastes, huge industrial activities every year, spread millions of tons of pollutants into the air. The immediate results appear as irritations to the throat and eyes of the city dweller; in the country vegetation is damaged; rivers are polluted.

Sulphur dioxide is one of the chief foes. On contact with moisture, it easily becomes sulphuric acid. Civic legislation is struggling with the problem of dirty air, which wraps itself around our cities. Yet the levels of sulphur dioxide continue to rise with the growth of industry. In large industrial cities in Europe the air can contain twice as much sulphur dioxide as dirt.

In industrial cities in America, ozone is reaching danger level. Ozone is formed by a series of reactions which involve the exhaust gases from automobiles and sunlight. Ozone will destroy cellulose and cause deterioration with rubber and many organic materials.

The cumulative mess from all this pollution contains a number of harmful chemicals that will wreak destruction on

Baize will prevent candlesticks scratching furniture

our possessions and homes. With many works of art the damage may not appear for some time, but inevitably delicate patinas and paint films will be marred as pollutants settle. Fabrics will lose their strength. Leather will weaken and paper will be affected.

Inside and outside grimy deposits are laid. They soil everything. Laundry, cleaning and painting bills rise. A walk down the street can show, all too clearly, how even the hardest building material is being etched away, until, in some cases, the original detail and design has almost disappeared.

The last two decades have brought to our notice yet another enemy. Traffic volume has increased alarmingly and the percentage of giant lorries has grown. Thirty-ton monsters rumble and roar with pounding diesel engines past our houses, through villages and cities. This vibration and con- cussion from heavy traffic is storming its way across the

Chimneys pour 1,500,000 tons of smoke, grit and dust into the atmosphere each year

landscape and has already left behind a legacy of cracks and damage in houses, cathedrals and historic buildings.

But under the heading of transport there is a more sinister customer and one that is largely unpredictable at the moment. The rumbling sonic boom from ultra-fast aircraft is starting to make itself felt.

Concussion and noise are not only a menace to the works of our culture but ultimately to us all, as they rise to a crescendo in our sound-ridden era.

Events such as the inundation of Florence and the present condition in Venice are made worse by pollutants. In Florence beautiful white Carrara marble statues were veiled with fuel oil. Paintings were coated with the same, and chemicals such as naphtha attacked colours and surfaces. In Venice, exquisite architecture appears to be melting away under the combined onslaught of time and the insidious agents of the twentieth century.

The effects of centuries of air pollution on the Vierge Dorée, Amiens cathedral

## Security against theft

There is still one department of care that should be considered. This is security against theft. Strangely enough, this is a field which is regarded with apathy by many householders. If you ask a policeman, he will be only too ready to confirm that stories of open windows and unlocked doors are not fairy-tales, but hard facts.

How do you set about pulling up the drawbridge? A first step can be to put yourself in the place of an intruder. Wander round your property and see how many chinks you can find; a ladder left against a wall or kept out of doors; a window left purposely unsecured, in case you forget your key; a key left in a letterbox with a tell-tale piece of string hanging outside – secret places for keys, such as under doormats or on shelves in a garage, can generally be discovered by the crook.

As a first line of defence provide secure fastenings for doors and windows. Doors should be inspected for warping and if possible, be fitted into a frame that overlaps and makes it difficult to work on the lock. Many cylinder locks that rely on a spring-held bolt are all too easy to open. There are however, in this category, locks that by a reverse action of the key become a deadlock that cannot be opened either from the outside or the inside without the key. Even more secure can be a multi-lever mortice deadlock. If mechanisms of these types are fitted, it means that the burglar will have to make a lot of noise as he breaks down enough of the door to make an entry. If further security is needed, adequate bolts at the top and bottom of the door can be fitted inside, and it is certainly a wise move to include a stout door-chain that will allow for the inspection of unknown callers without completely unsecuring the door. Better still for this purpose is to have an optical peephole at eye-level.

Sash windows with their normal fastenings are easy meat. It only needs the blade of a stout knife and the latch can be silently swung across. A simple course here is to fit window bolts that will securely fasten both halves of the window in the closed position. There are locks and safety fastenings that can be fitted to casement windows and they are a good

How would you burgle this house?

Simple locks are often easy to open, especially when the door fits loosely

investment. If you secure windows and doors to the best of your ability, you are a long way towards defeating the burglar because, as the police will tell you, the large majority of criminals do not like to chance breaking glass or making a noise.

Science is fast moving into the fight against theft. In many countries there are now a fair number of firms who make it a speciality to safeguard homes and valuables. Often for quite moderate sums devices such as pressure pads that can be put under door mats, and in other strategic places, can be installed, and they are a particular headache to the crook, as generally he will be quite unaware of their where-abouts. More sophisticated equipment includes radar and invisible rays. For large halls there are highly sensitive microwave intruder detectors which will react to even a slight movement up to fifty yards away. There is one particular gadget in this class that can be programmed only to react to human movement characteristics.

These warning devices can be triggered to sound bells, but more and more it is becoming the custom to have them connected to the police station. They may have a tape recorder attachment which, once the security system has been penetrated, immediately rings the police and tells them the address of the property that is being attacked.

Newspapers and magazines very often have articles detailing the latest thefts. It is of interest to study these. The results can be illuminating. Although many high-priced objects are taken, there seems to be a marked increase in the removal of quite mundane pieces that one would hardly think it was worth stealing. All this points to the fact that a proper inventory of the house's contents should be made. Reputable insurance companies will usually ask for this, probably stating that they would like a description of those objects over a certain value.

The preparation of an inventory will take time, and it is advisable to back it up with illustrative evidence; for example, if you have a piece of Wedgwood and it has some small imperfections, a sketch should be made indicating where chips or cracks are. If you have a silver bowl that may have a small dent, abrasions or other marks, it should be treated in the same way.

A screw bolt will secure the vulnerable sash window

Uncancelled milk and newspapers advertise that the house is empty

Sketches and written descriptions should certainly be backed up with photographs, which can be black and white, but with many pieces it is better if the photographs are in colour. The objects should preferably be photographed against a plain background, as they will stand out better. It does not take very long to rig up a temporary studio. A white sheet can be hung down the wall and across a table on which the objects can be stood. Take the photographs as close up as the size of the objects and the lens of your camera will allow. When you have done all this, you have provided yourself with evidence, and also factual information to guide the police.

If there is one single feature that probably helps the crook more than any other, it is publicity. It is a very simple matter for him to attend a major sale and to make notes of the values of the objects and who buys what and where the people live. It is also known that the crook will spend time studying the social columns in papers and magazines. These often very helpfully announce the movements of owners, saying that they will be leaving their home to spend a lengthy holiday, possibly a thousand miles away.

Be careful also with handbags and briefcases, particularly if they contain keys and evidence of your identity and address. The following incident illustrates this point. A handbag was stolen from a woman in a large store. She naturally told the management and then went off to her home, which was some twenty miles away. The following day she was rung up by someone purporting to be the manager, who said that her handbag had been recovered and would she come to collect it. She said she would come right away. When she got to the store no-one knew anything of such a 'phone call, nor had her bag been found. When she returned home she had been robbed.

As a small simple tailpiece, do not forget to cancel the milk and the newspapers when you go away.

Photographs and a detailed written description will help police

# RECIPES

## Beeswax Polish

Beeswax . . . . . . . . . . . . . . . 4 ounces
Turpentine . . . . . . . . . . . . . 12 fluid ounces

The beeswax should be melted in a tin and whilst it is still liquid the turpentine should be stirred in. Fire precautions should be taken. If less turpentine is added, the polish will be stiffer. If a thinner polish is needed, increase the proportion of turpentine. If a lighter coloured polish is needed, purified white beeswax should be used instead of yellow. This polish can be used not only for wood, but also for bronze, iron, steel, and leather.

## Furniture Cream

Purified white beeswax . . . . 3 ounces
Turpentine . . . . . . . . . . . . . 8 ounces
Water . . . . . . . . . . . . . . . . . 8 ounces

Melt the beeswax, remove from heat and pour in the turpentine, followed by the water, which should be hot. Stirring constantly, add a few drops of ammonia, which will thicken the mixture to a cream.

## Furniture Cleaner

Turpentine . . . . . . . . . . . . . 3 parts
Linseed Oil . . . . . . . . . . . . . 3 parts
Vinegar . . . . . . . . . . . . . . . 2 parts

Put all the ingredients into a bottle and shake well before use. There is very little solvent power in this, so that it should not harm the underlying polish.

## Wax-sticks

Beeswax . . . . . . . . . . . . . . . 3 ounces
Paraffin-wax . . . . . . . . . . . . 1 ounce

Melt the two waxes together. Remove from heat and quickly stir in dry powder colours for the tint of your choice. With this amount of the waxes, one level teaspoonful of the powder colours should be sufficient. It can be poured into a rectangular shallow tin, and when nearly set, cut into pieces with a knife.

Fitted military dressing case, of about 1820

## British Museum Leather Dressing

Anhydrous lanolin . . . . . . . . 7 ounces
Beeswax . . . . . . . . . . . . . . . . half ounce
Cedarwood oil . . . . . . . . . . . 1 fluid ounce
Hexane . . . . . . . . . . . . . . . . 11 fluid ounces

Fire precautions must be taken, as the hexane is highly inflammable. First shred the beeswax into the hexane and shake until dissolved. Then add the lanolin and the cedar-

Early nineteenth-century American candle shades

wood oil. It should be shaken thoroughly before use.

## Water or Heat Marks on Furniture (1)

Olive oil . . . . . . . . . . . . . . . 4 fluid ounces
Paraffin wax . . . . . . . . . . . . 1 ounce

Put the two together and heat until the wax has melted. To use, rub sparingly on the marks. Leave for half an hour and wipe off. Repeat if necessary.

## Water or Heat Marks on Furniture (2)

Linseed oil . . . . . . . . . . . . . 12 fluid ounces
Turpentine . . . . . . . . . . . . . 3 fluid ounces

Taking fire precautions, simmer the linseed oil for fifteen minutes. When cool, add the turpentine. Shake before use and apply quite plentifully with a piece of cotton wool. Leave the cotton wool and liquid in place overnight. Wipe off and repolish.

## Silver Teapot Cleaner

When there is tannin staining inside, this can be removed by pouring into the pot a pint of hot water to which half an ounce of borax has been added. Leave the pot to stand for an hour. Then gently scrub the inside with a soft brush. Empty and rinse several times. (This remedy can also be used for a coffee-stained silver pot.)

## Stain Removal from Decanters

If the recipes for this in the text are not efficacious, the following can be tried:

1) Half a pint of water, to which has been added a tablespoonful of household ammonia.

2) Half a pint of water to which has been added two tablespoonsful of domestic bleach.

After both these applications, several thorough rinsings should be given.

## Grease Stains on Carpets

A fastness test should be made and then a thick paste of fuller's earth and water should be spread over the stain. It can then be left to dry and finally brushed out.

## Mildew Marks on Fabrics

Mix a creamy paste with whiting and dilute ammonia. Spoon this over the marks and leave for five minutes. Remove. Observe progress. If necessary repeat. Then rinse thoroughly.

## Bloom on Polished Furniture

This is caused generally by polishing over a wet surface. To cure, the top polish must be taken off with turpentine, or white spirit. The piece should be thoroughly dried and then repolished.

## Tarnish from Copper

Vinegar  . . . . . . . . . . . . . . . 4 fluid ounces
Salt  . . . . . . . . . . . . . . . . . . . . 1 ounce

Shake together and apply with a soft rag. Rinse thoroughly, and then use a standard metal polish. Finish with a soft duster.

# GLOSSARY

**Alabaster,** a type of gypsum of fine texture. Usually it is white and translucent. It may have tints of yellow, grey or red, caused by impurities. It is generally used for carving small figures, ornaments and vases

**Amboyna wood,** an imported timber used for veneers and inlays in the eighteenth century

**Aqua fortis,** nitric acid. This is used in a diluted form for etching

**Aquatint,** an etching process which uses areas of tone rather than line. A copper or zinc plate is grounded with specks of resin or asphaltum. The tone area created by the repetitive use of stopping-out varnish

**Artist's proof,** one of a limited edition of prints from an etching plate, a steel engraving or a block print. These are signed by the artist and they are generally numbered; for example, figures 3/30 would mean that it is the third print taken of an edition of thirty

**Benzene,** a solvent from coal-tar. It is highly inflammable and poisonous and should not be used

**Benzine,** solvent similar to petrol. It is safe for cleaning fabrics

**Biscuit,** a ceramic term that implies that a piece of pottery has been fired without a glaze and left like this as a finish

**Britannia metal,** a form of pewter that was made harder by adding antimony and copper. Its use commenced at the beginning of the nineteenth century

**Burin,** a tool used by an engraver. Its head may be lozenge, square or U-shaped

**Carnauba wax,** one of the hardest waxes. It comes from the Brazilian palm. It can be used as an ingredient with lacquers, polishes and varnishes

**Cartoon,** in the fine art sense this implies a full-scale brush or pencil drawing for an easel painting, a mural or a tapestry

**Fire brat,** a tiny insect, something like a silver-fish, which can cause damage particularly to books. It feeds on the pastes or glues in the bindings

**Fixative,** a liquid that is sprayed on to a pastel, charcoal or soft pencil drawings to hold them. Early fixatives were made of shellac dissolved in methylated spirit. Those used today are synthetic cellulose solutions

**French polish,** a high gloss surface produced by applications of shellac dissolved in alcohol, with sometimes other resins being added. Its use began in the nineteenth century

**Hardwood,** dyed sycamore that was used for inlay and veneer work in the eighteenth century

**Lacquer,** a yellow varnish made from shellac dissolved in alcohol. It can be coloured with pigments. It has a high gloss and a very hard brittle film. Today its use on metals has been superseded by cellulose and other synthetic liquids

A fine old gramophone at the Flea Market in Brussels

Are they genuine? Can I afford it? London's Portobello Road market

**Marouflage,** the fixing of a canvas to a panel or wall surface. The usual cement is white lead with linseed oil; glues and wax adhesives are also used

**Marquetry,** the decoration of furniture by laying coloured woods in the same manner as veneer. Other substances such as ivory, metal and tortoise-shell can be used

**Mezzotint,** a print produced from a copper, zinc or steel plate, that has had its surface first roughened by a special tool. The highlights and details are then scraped and burnished into this surface. The process was invented by Ludwig von Siegen in about 1640

**Monotype,** a print that is taken from a plate on which the picture has been painted with brush and colours, also pen and ink pictures. As the name suggests, only one print can be made of each picture

**Niello,** the art of chasing out lines or forms in silver which are then inlaid with a black composition called 'nigellum'

**Parquetry,** a laid or veneer method for the decoration of furniture using wood of the same colour, but obtaining the effect by contrasting the directions of the grain

**Pinchbeck,** an alloy of copper and zinc popular in the eighteenth century for the production of cheap jewellery

**Polychrome,** applied to sculpture it implies that the piece is, or was, painted

A junk sale in the United States

**Retouching varnish,** a light natural resin or synthetic resin varnish which can be used very soon after an oil painting has been completed, so that the artist can assess his work. It is so thin that it will not cause cracking

**Serigraph,** a print taken by using a silk screen on which some form of stencil has been placed. The ink is forced through the screen on to the paper by the use of a squeegee

**Sugar aquatint,** the design is painted on to the copper or zinc plate with a mixture of black, gamboge, sugar and a little water. Stopping-out varnish is brushed over the plate which is then left in a bath of cold water until the water penetrates the varnish and causes the black paint to swell and lift the varnish off. The plate is then etched

**Tempera,** a picture painted in true tempera has the pigments mixed with fresh raw egg-yolk

**Terracotta,** a term derived from the Italian for 'baked earth'. It is unglazed and has a warm reddish or brownish colour

**Tint tool,** a triangular sectioned graver which produces very fine lines in wood engraving

**Triptych,** a picture which may be one of a series or a single composition painted on three leaves. The two outer ones fold together for protection

**Vellum,** originally calf-gut, later calf skin. It was treated like parchment. It was also the name for a vegetable composition made to resemble the real thing

**Water marks,** distinguishing marks which are impressed on sheets of paper during manufacture. They show initials, dates, and trademarks. They first appeared in European papers at the end of the thirteenth century

# BOOKS TO READ

*Watch and Clock Making and Repairing* by W. J. Gazeley. Butterworth, London, 1970.

*Furniture Doctor* by George Grotz. Barrie & Jenkins, London, 1969.

*Care of Antiques* by John FitzMaurice Mills. Arlington Books, London, 1964.

*Pergamon Dictionary of Art* by John FitzMaurice Mills. Pergamon Press, Oxford, 1965.

*Picture Cleaning and Restoration* by John FitzMaurice Mills. Winsor & Newton, London, 1966.

*Repairing Books* by G. S. Percival. Dryad Press, Leicester, n.d.

*Preservation of Leather Bookbindings* by H. J. Plenderleith. British Museum, London, 1970.

*Repairing and Restoring China and Glass* by William Karl Klein. Harper & Row, London, 1962.

*Mending and Restoring China* by Thomas Pond. Garnstone Press, London, 1970.

*Refurbishing Antiques* by Rosemary Ratcliff. Pelham Books, London, 1971.

*The Art and Antique Restorers' Handbook* by George Savage. Barrie & Rockliff, London, 1968.

# INDEX

# ACKNOWLEDGEMENTS

Bethnal Green Museum, London 41
**Claude Gallery, London**: front cover
Courtesy of Messrs. Sotheby, London 4, 5
Courtesy of the Trustees of the British Museum 45
Dalva Brothers Inc. New York 138
Foto Marburg 47
Hamlyn Group Picture Library 31, 74, 142, 149, 150
Los Angeles County Museum of Art 31
Metropolitan Museum of Art, New York (Jos. V. McMullan Collection) 24
Picturepoint Ltd. London 153, 154, 155
Piercebridge Antiques Ltd 12
Popperfoto, London 140, 141
Victoria & Albert Museum, London 38
Vita Juel, London 13

The author also wishes to give grateful acknowledgement to the following for their permission to reproduce various illustrations in the book: Christie's, The Cottage of Content, The National Museum of Ireland, N. R. Omell, Perez Ltd.

WARNING: When using acetone, always be certain that there is ample ventilation.

# SOME OTHER TITLES IN THIS SERIES

■ **Arts**
Antique Furniture/Architecture/Art Nouveau for Collectors/Clocks and Watches/Glass for Collectors/Jewellery/Musical Instruments/Porcelain/Pottery/Silver for Collectors/Victoriana

■ **Domestic Animals and Pets**
Budgerigars/Cats/Dog Care/Dogs/Horses and Ponies/Pet Birds/Pets for Children/Tropical Freshwater Aquaria/Tropical Marine Aquaria

■ **Domestic Science**
Flower Arranging

■ **Gardening**
Chrysanthemums/Garden Flowers/Garden Shrubs/House Plants/Plants for Small Gardens/Roses

■ **General Information**
Aircraft/Arms and Armour/Coins and Medals/Espionage/Flags/Fortune Telling/Freshwater Fishing/Guns/Military Uniforms/Motor Boats and Boating/National Costumes of the world/Orders and Decorations/Rockets and Missiles/Sailing/Sailing Ships and Sailing Craft/Sea Fishing/Trains/Veteran and Vintage Cars/Warships

■ **History and Mythology**
Age of Shakespeare/Archaeology/Discovery of: Africa/The American West/Australia/Japan/North America/South America/Great Land Battles/Great Naval Battles/Myths and Legends of: Africa/Ancient Egypt/Ancient Greece/Ancient Rome/India/The South Seas/Witchcraft and Black Magic

■ **Natural History**
The Animal Kingdom/Animals of Australia and New Zealand/Animals of Southern Asia/Bird Behaviour/Birds of Prey/Butterflies/Evolution of Life/Fishes of the world/Fossil Man/A Guide to the Seashore/Life in the Sea/Mammals of the world/Monkeys and Apes/Natural History Collecting/The Plant Kingdom/Prehistoric Animals/Seabirds/Seashells/Snakes of the world/Trees of the world/Tropical Birds/Wild Cats

■ **Popular Science**
Astronomy/Atomic Energy/Chemistry/Computers at Work/The Earth/Electricity/Electronics/Exploring the Planets/Heredity/The Human Body/Mathematics/Microscopes and Microscopic Life/Physics/Psychology/Undersea Exploration/The Weather Guide